experienced intense hurting

essays on self-esteem

By L.S. Barksdale

THE BARKSDALE FOUNDATION
Publishers

53625 Double View Drive, PO Box 187
Idyllwild, California 92349 (714) 659-3858

contents

essays on self-esteem

preface

I began my life on a cattle ranch in the heart of the Colorado Rockies and was graduated from Colorado State University in the depth of the great depression of 1929 with a Bachelor of Science degree in mechanical engineering. In order to support myself and my family, I did various manual and semi-skilled work on new road construction and worked as a general mechanic and high line rigger on three dam construction jobs. I also worked as a brakeman, "chuck tender" and "gandy dancer" on the Colorado River Aqueduct. I really thought I had it made when I finally succeeded in landing my first engineering job with a major oil company in the fall of 1935. I was sadly disillusioned when the company's new chief engineer called me into his office one day early in the recession of 1937. He not only fired me but told me: "Barksdale, you just don't have what it takes to get ahead in the world. You had better get some routine job and be content with it." My already abysmally low self-esteem really hit bottom and I had no place to go but "up."

Feeling very unworthy and "less than," I experienced a desperate and compulsive need to prove my worth through my achievements — not then realizing that my very existence proves my innate worth and importance. With such intense motivation, I opened a successful engineering and development firm and later became the co-partner and president of a business that furnished over 80 per cent of the hydraulic control valves used on U.S. aircraft, both military and commercial. I also became the co-partner of the largest costume jewelry manufacturer West of the Mississippi.

Disposing of my interest in these firms, I founded three other highly successful firms which did a thriving business throughout the free world. I developed a revolutionary valving principle and pioneered extreme pressure fluid controls for both aircraft and industry. Among other accomplishments, I designed and built highly specialized valves for the Nautilus, the first atomic powered submarine, after other valve companies had given up.

In spite of my material success and, although the recipient of numerous honors and awards, I found, to my dismay, that my intense feeling of inferiority and unworthiness had in no way diminished. What was wrong? Hadn't I shown both my past critics and myself that I was a success in both engineering and business?

Finally, my continuing deep sense of inferiority and unworthiness caused me to question my values and frantic life style and to embark on an intense search for self-understanding. There followed years of unhappiness, of penetrating self-probing and observation accompanied by agonizing migraine headaches, high blood pressure, ulcers, arthritis and finally a heart attack.

My desperate and ceaseless search, however, gradually opened insights into the cause of my years of intense hurting and unhappiness. To my amazement, I discovered that I had been attempting to live a normal, happy life in a world of impossibly high standards erected by myself and society, in a compulsive effort to prove my worth. In this strange and unreal world anything less than perfection was inadequate and blameworthy, and thus a cause for deep feelings of inferiority, shame and guilt. I strove so hard to meet my unreasonable standards of performance that I achieved a high measure of material success but was continually plagued with accompanying physical ailments. Neither did I achieve the genuine "feel good" I have since found is everyone's birthright. For no matter how hard I tried, or how well I did, I never felt I had done "well enough." Thus, I was never able to overcome my extreme sense of inadequacy, inferiority and self-rejection.

I was in a continual state of emotional turmoil and hurting and finally realized that, without a drastic change in my concepts and values, I would never be able to "feel good." This realization sparked a desperate search for the solution to my self-rejection and hurting. The resulting insights made it abundantly clear that all my self-accusation, shame, guilt and remorse — my sense of unworthiness and feeling "less than" every time I made a mistake — my extreme unhappiness — was the product of faulty cultural conditioning.

Once I was able to discover the false concepts of human behavior which perpetuated my unhappiness and hurting and which, I also discovered were totally invalid, I was able to replace them with concepts in alignment with the realities observable in human behavior. It was then I realized that my very existence proves my worth and importance, and that I could in no way improve my worth by my accomplishments. This realization enabled me to achieve true success — that is, happiness in my personal life.

These insights revolutionized my life and in 1964 motivated me to dispose of my business interests, both at home and abroad, in order to devote the balance of my life to helping people achieve Sound Self-Esteem, which is genuine love of self. This is done by enabling them to get rid of their false and destructive concepts and replace them with the observable realities of human behavior.

My greatest motivation, however, for contributing my energy and fortune to this endeavor is the clear realization that children yet unborn will suffer as I have suffered, through the destructive life style passed on from generation to generation by parents with low Self-Esteem. Unless this vicious cycle is broken, we will have more and more battered children, parent-child alienation, suicides, crime in the streets, an ever-increasing welfare load, more overflowing prisons and mental health institutions, more and more alcohol and drug abuse centers and an ever more staggering divorce rate — all stemming from a hurting or crippling lack of Self-Esteem — from the self-rejection resulting from a false sense of inadequacy, inferiority and worthlessness.

To this end I founded The Barksdale Foundation, a non-profit, self-funding institution For Furtherance of Human Understanding, I cite my own personal experience as evidence of the dynamic effectiveness of its Self-Esteem Program. At 68, after many years of both emotional and physical pain, the death of both my only son and cherished wife and other devastating personal problems, I feel better mentally, physically and emotionally than I have ever felt in my life.

The essays collected in this book evolved over a period of years. The first, "My Perception of Reality," was written in 1964. While there is repetition of the basic message, the essays in historical perspective show the emergence of new insights into the problems of our faulty cultural conditioning. Each essay attacks the problem from a slightly different angle. I hope these essays will motivate you to achieve Sound Self-Esteem, for I have discovered that with Sound Self-Esteem, success and happiness are inevitable.

May the blessings of Sound Self-Esteem be yours all the days of your life.

— L.S. "Barks" Barksdale
January, 1977

essays on
self-esteem

MY PERCEPTION OF REALITY

I offer my perception of reality (not simply intellectual concepts but the way I actually sense life) that it may spark others to clarify their own basic convictions, fully realizing that what is true for me may or may not be true for another. Of vital importance is that each determines what is "right" for him. For only thus can we achieve innner freedom, peace and happiness.

L.S. Barksdale

I perceive the *very core of life* to be *infinite, undifferentiated consciousness;*
That everything that exists is a differentiated part of this formless consciousness
And experience its simple and eternal ISness — its power and beneficence,
Forever ready to express through man and evident throughout his environment.

I am aware that man is an individualized center of this infinite consciousness,
Innately precious and unique, eternal and inviolable — limited only by his wisdom and love,
In varying stages of awareness of his own reality and of the laws and forces of life;
That he has an unrelenting cosmic urge to express that he may discover
His wonder and greatness in his trial-and-error search for enlightenment;
And that every instant he is doing the *very best his current awareness permits.*

I perceive that man's egocentric drives are a desperate groping for self-acceptance
And that "good and evil" are but manifestations of his level of knowing;
That life on earth is but a fleeting instant in our totality,
And that death is but the release from a halting material existence
That we may progress into a new phase of learning and growth;
That regardless of appearances nothing occurs without meaning and purpose.

I realize that *the meaning of life is to grow in wisdom and love;*
Not to be "more" than others but simply to become more aware of our reality
And experience the fantastic wonder and richness of living in the NOW
In the deep realization that *we are ONE* with infinite consciousness.
I perceive that only when we truly love and value ourselves are we able to
Free ourselves of frustration, inadequacy and fear, of enmity, envy and aggression
And tune in to the subtle all-prevading love, wisdom and power of the universe.

1

I am aware of the fundamental simplicity, harmony and rightness of life;
That *love is its essence, growth its purpose* and *joy its realization;*
That it is we, who through our ignorance, cause its seeming complexity and misery.
I apprehend that we cannot be separated from our source, infinite consciousness,
For the underlying truth of existence *is* that *man IS differentiated consciousness.*

Though compassionate and eager to help, I am unshaken by human error and suffering,
Knowing each is expanding his awareness according to his own specific needs
And that man is interrelated in unrealized needs as well as in his consciousness.
I know that although I neither want nor can live unto myself alone, my primary responsibility is my own growth and well-being;
That only through my own understanding can I help others in search of peace and freedom, of truth and love.

I realize that I am immune to human judgment and *can transcend my conditioning.*
I know that every instant, *everything is right* for my needed learning and growth
And that our environment can hurt us only as much as we ourselves permit;
That we *can* alter the cause and effect relationships that shape our lives,
And that we have all the time there is for our individual unfoldment.

I perceive man to be infinitely more than he appears to be
And capable of a great deal more than intellectual jousting with his environment;
That he can DO anything he can imagine, believe and *sense* himself doing.
But *above all* he need be AWARE, *and true to his inner urgings*
If he is to experience the peace of self-acceptance and the love of his fellowmen.

THE ANATOMY OF CHOICE

It is rare indeed that a person perceives his own true worth. One cannot, then, come even close to achieving his fantastic potential, for water can no more rise above its source than we can exceed our own evaluation and expectations. To do a thing *we must first believe it is possible.* Most of us have such a poor opinion of our worth and ability that we not only severely limit our accomplishments but suffer the psychological misery of crippling inferiority and self-rejection. In fact, we may actually hate ourselves for our fancied inadequacies. And in a futile attempt to escape from a self which *we* consider inferior, if not indeed too worthless to exist, we often turn to compulsive over-indulgence in food, alcohol, sex, or drugs. Or we may try to lose ourselves in constant frenzied activity. We may also suffer severe depression, mental aberration—even resort to suicide. Moreover, something in our nature *forces us to act in accordance with this self-conjured image.* Others, consequently, can only accept our own damaging valuation, thus confirming and reinforcing our limited self-estimate.

The basic cause of our inability to accept ourselves at our real value is *condemnation* by ourselves and others for doing or being *"less"* or *"worse"* than we *"should."* Condemnation is so ingrained in our culture that even small children quickly lose their freshness and spontaneity and erect protective barriers to isolate them from the pain and hurt of personal censure. Thus one's sensitivity, so precious to open and rich relationships, is lost—rarely to be regained.

Contrary to what many believe, condemnation *is not* desirable or necessary for our self-improvement and growth. What *is* necessary is first to recognize that we have made a mistake, and then to engage in honest self-inquiry in order to determine just how and why we made it. For it is only thru *understanding the cause and recognizing the effect* of an error that we can cease making it. Otherwise we only create self-defeating conflict and resistance. Condemnation is further detrimental to our growth and development, for in order to avoid the guilt, shame and remorse resulting from personal criticism, we usually try to *ignore or justify our mistakes* rather than simply recognizing them and searching within for the causes.

Moreover, self-criticism causes much resentment, hostility and unhappiness in our inter-personal relationships. For we censure others in order to minimize our own mistakes and to relieve the discomfort and hurt of our own condemnation. And we can no more accept and love others while hating and rejecting ourselves than an apple can fall skyward.

Self-condemnation is *totally bad,* i.e. entirely non-productive, distintegrating, and destructive of our wellbeing and happiness. It negates the fact that what a person *is* is distinctly different from what a person *does.* For at the central core of our being we are each precious, unique and inviolable; whereas what a person does, regardless of his errors, is but a manifestation of his unfolding maturity. And if we could but accept ourselves free of condemnation—if we could but *condemn the act without condemning the person* who committed it—we would then drop our emotional resistance and intelligently effect the changes desirable for a more productive and harmonious life.

Probably man's greatest non-physical need is *self-acceptance and approval.* However, we prevent its fulfillment by our continual self-condemnation. Consequently, in a vain and desperate effort to satisfy this inherent need we endeavor to gain the approval of others, often through irrational and foolish acts. Actually, however, we can only achieve a satisfying self-image through our *own* unconditional acceptance and the realization that we do not necessarily have to like *everything* we do. For we each have our individual growth pattern—"our own way to go." Although this intense drive for recognition and approval is normally misinterpreted as evidence of a wanton self-love and roundly censured as egoistic, it is in fact motivated by our very *lack* of self-acceptance and genuine self-love. For if we were truly satisfied with our self-image—if we really liked ourselves—we would not be dependent on others' acceptance and approval for our stability and emotional wellbeing.

Cursory examination discloses that condemnation arises from our minute-to-minute and day-to-day decisions and their subsequent actions. It is, therefore, to our *choices* that we must look for relief from this burden of condemnation. Such a search is crucially important, for lack of acceptance and approval of one's self is the root cause of our human predicament.

Fortunately it is possible to relieve this burden. To do so, however, it is absolutely necessary to muster an *open mind,* to suspend judgment and to hold in abeyance our preconceived assumptions and conclusions. If we can thus objectively examine *just how and why* we make a specific choice, we will perceive that *all condemnation is completely unjustified,* from either a moral or rational point of view. Such a realization will permit us to achieve a keen awareness and free us to unfold our inherent potential, thus allowing us to live a much happier, more productive life.

"Then there was the fellow who had such strong will power he was unable to stop smoking. He told himself he wanted to quit smoking but found that his will was so strong it wouldn't let him." Strangely enough, this joke is very close to reality, as we shall see.

A decision or choice is made in one of the three following ways, depending on our degree of maturity.

1. An unconscious choice, which is simply a reaction to prevailing stimuli in accordance with the conditioned habits and values arising from our environment, such as the unthinking and impulsive reactions to our desires of the moment.

2. A conscious choice determined by the deliberate application of our prevailing perception and wisdom to the problem at hand. This requires a questioning pause prior to any decision and action while the problem is sensed, and alternative solutions developed and evaluated.

3. A decision or choice made directly and intuitively from our inner knowing, as in the case of a "hunch," which, if genuine and not merely wishful thinking, is infallible.

The first is of course by far our most common type of choice and the second, which may also contain elements of the first and third, is the next most common. However, the rightness of any choice or decision depends on our individual understanding and adequate consideration of all the relevant factors. The factors entering into and determining *any* reaction or conscious decision are:

1. Our current stage of perception and wisdom, i.e., our awareness and understanding.

2. Our basic needs, such as our inherent need to express and our desperate need for acceptance, to "belong" and to love and be loved.

3. The total conditioning of our experience and environment, which has determined our concepts, attitudes, beliefs, values, prejudices, desires, habit patterns, goals, etc.

4. Our prevailing emotions resulting from our needs and conditioning, such as love, hate, fear, anger, envy, jealousy, frustration, hostility, aggression, compassion, impatience, etc.

5. The current pressures of our environment.

6. Inner, often unknown, urges arising from our stored data and our intuition.

7. Our factual knowledge of the specific situation or condition.

8. Our mental acumen.

9. Our prevailing health and energy level.

5

At the instant of any decision man's prevailing perception and wisdom automatically integrate his needs, urges, values, beliefs, desires and factual data, at all levels of his understanding, and they then come up with the best decision that he can mentally generate and can emotionally and physically afford. And, while the above nine factors are in a continual state of flux, at the *instant of decision* they are absolutely fixed, just as the click of a shutter freezes and captures a flash of action on the film.

In light of the above it is a self-evident fact that *every* decision or choice is invariably the best that that particular individual can possibly make at that particular instant in time. For it is absolutely *the only possible decision* he can arrive at with his prevailing understanding, all the pertinent factors being fixed at that specific instant.

The logic of the foregoing observations now makes apparent a most fundamental and vital truth, namely this: man has absolutely no justification for condemning himself or his fellowman for any choice or action, however much it may be out of alignment, i.e. bad, evil, sinful, stupid, etc. For could we look at the problem with an open and unconditioned mind we would readily see that any given decision was inevitable. Thus all shame, blame, guilt and remorse are completely unfounded, and are indeed foolish. Such a realization enables us to recognize and deal with the negative facts of a given situation without condemnation.

Just as surely as no sale is made without the consent of the buyer, no personal action takes place until a particular desire is so strong that the person cannot resist its urge for fulfillment. This we call motivation and it is absolutely the only reason for any decision or action. "Will," except as a synonym for desire or wish, is a complete fallacy and myth. There is simply no such thing as a "sheer act of will" regardless of what we may read or think. For, contrary to what is commonly accepted, we invariably act only according to the motivation that our understanding generates thru integration of the above nine factors, and *not* thru some mysterious "will power" that a person of "strong character" is able to command when our mores and prevailing circumstances so indicate. Thus it is much more appropriate to refer to our power of decision as "desire power" rather than "will power" since it is clear from the foregoing analysis of choice that, all factors considered, *we invariably do what we most want to do.* Or in other words, *we always do exactly the one thing that we would rather do than not do.* And this observation on how and why we act is invariably true whether or not the action is acceptable in our culture.

It is now obvious that, owing to the inexorable law of cause and effect, a person is inevitably the product of all his past thought and action and thus of his unfolding understanding. It is therefore of the utmost importance that we make every effort to expand our consciousness if we are to so tailor our motivation that we act in alignment with life. And since a price is exacted for every decision we make it is essential that we ascertain that price so that we can intelligently decide whether or not we can afford and are willing to pay it. For it is only by either intuitive or wise conscious choice that we can live in harmony with our inner selves and our total environment.

It is also evident from the foregoing that our entire system of reward and punishment is completely invalid. For while *man is inescapably subject to the consequences of his choices and actions,* despite his lack of understanding, he is never justly subject to condemnation in our hearts for his lack of greater wisdom. And thus, though he may have to be physically restrained for the protection of society, neither he nor his acts can ever justify punishment as such. Since the harmony and rightness of any decision depend on one's current perception and wisdom, the only just and practical solution to his problem of misalignment is to motivate him to self-discovery and to aid him in furthering his understanding. The basic need of the anti-social person is to apprehend reality and thereby achieve alignment with life, that he may eventually live in harmony with himself and his fellowman.

And though we may recognize or perhaps respect and admire a person for courage, exemplary moral and prudent actions etc., arising from his high degree of understanding, it is obviously entirely unwarranted to reward or worship him for such God-given ability, for no one can raise himself by his bootstraps. We are all limited by, and only by, our current degree of knowing. For even our concepts, attitudes, beliefs, values, desires, goals and emotions are but manifestations of our degree of understanding and we cannot rise above them except thru expanding our awareness and wisdom.

But in order to expand our understanding that we may eventually experience the potential well-being, peace and freedom inherent in achieving alignment with life, we must first be made aware of such need and thus be motivated to self-discovery. Knowledge, not wisdom, is to be found in books and sermons. To find wisdom we must look inward in order to question and to digest the lessons of our environment. It is through trial and error, observation and self-inquiry into our problems and our moment-to-moment and day-to-day relations with our fellowmen, and into the cause-and-effect relationships of our total environment, that we enhance our perception and unfold our God-given wisdom.

It is now apparent that we invariably choose what we most want to do at any particular instant, even though the choice may be against our self-interest, long-range goals or ideals. The only possible way we can bring such a choice into alignment with our more vital needs is to pause and, through a careful evaluation of the costs and benefits involved, revise our motivation accordingly.

A careful look at this operation, however, makes it clear that in order to make such a change we must deliberately take the time and have the perception to realize that: first, the proposed choice is actually against our self-interest; second, we must have sufficient desire to change our prevailing motivation; and third, the other conditions requisite for the desired change must be present.

While it is apparent, therefore, that we can consciously revise a preliminary choice, provided that we have the required motivation and the required conditions, it is equally obvious that we have no "free choice" in the usual sense of the term, since at the actual *instant of decision,* only *one* choice is possible.

Incidentally, this analysis explains why we so often eat, drink or smoke a great deal more than is good for us. For even though we may have sufficient perception to realize that such action is definitely against our self-interest, we are unable— owing to the previously itemized factors—to generate sufficient motivation to forego the immediate (and often illusory) benefits and proceed to the wiser choice. Thus *we invariably do the thing we would rather do than not do at the time.* Somewhat later, of course, owing to a change in one or more of the nine factors, our decision might be entirely different, albeit never "free."

Contrary to what the determinists believe, the possibilities of life are limitless. And even though we have no free choice as such, we are by no means automatons, pushed here and there by a willful fate. For we are each unique, and if so motivated, can take rich satisfaction in developing that uniqueness. Realizing that we are each limited by our individual understanding and being constantly pushed by an inherent urge to express ourselves, we can deliberately augment our self-knowledge and wisdom through keen observation of our own thought and action and an astute inquiry into our thinking and motivation. Thus, rather than torturing ourselves with destructive self-recrimination, we can profit from an objective and non-judgmental analysis of our unwise conduct, thereby advancing our learning and growth and improving our ability to cope with the various problems of our environment. And for those who are aware, there is the constant challenge: Do I have sufficient understanding to make a better decision?

In any event, we cannot *not* unfold, for life is dynamic and in a constant state of flux. And we, ourselves, are constantly changing and expanding our perception and wisdom through the action of the inexorable law of cause and effect, *whose consequences we cannot possibly escape.* Therefore, we inevitably learn and grow, for we profit or suffer according to the wisdom and alignment of our decisions. And although we act from conscious or unconscious choices derived from automatically-generated motivation rather than from "free will," we are yet—owing to our inherent drive to express ourselves—constantly improving our decision-making ability. Consequently, our acts are coming more and more into harmony with our inner selves, our fellowmen and our environment. The more deliberately we seek self-knowledge, however, the better we equip ourselves to make conscious wise choices and thus the more rapidly and less painfully we come into alignment with life.

L. S. BARKSDALE
12-4-64

SONG OF LIFE

Come, come out into the light,
Let the sun kiss your upturned face
And warm your soul.
Let the wind and the rain disclose you,
That your soul may stand free;
That the beauty that is you may be seen;
That you may glorify your Creator
By joining the inner and the outer
Into a seamless robe of joy and love.
Come out into the light, my beloved,
That I may rejoice and tremble in thy glory;
That we may both drink deeply of freedom
And slake our thirst of separateness.
Come out from the dark damp of despair,
For the air without is warm and balmy
And filled with a thousand delights,
Only waiting to bless and anoint thee.
Come, come out into the light, my beloved;
I too am incomplete without thee,
Without thy warmth and thy love.
I would share my joy and sadness,
My unwavering faith and exhilaration,
My tenderness and my love..

Lilburn S. Barksdale

11

I AM MY OWN AUTHORITY

The following statements acknowledge the fact that I must give myself the *right* to be *me* – to function as *I* see fit. These self-directives are crucially important to genuine self-appreciation and acceptance for they help release the emotional resistance and guilt arising from repression and the unconscious programming of our subconscious. It is impossible to have sound self-esteem until we are true to ourself and accept *full responsibility* for our own life – for fulfillment of our own needs.

I ALLOW MYSELF THE FREEDOM – I GIVE MYSELF THE RIGHT:

To recognize myself as the most important and interesting person in my world – a unique and precious part of life.

To feel warm and happy, kind and loving toward *myself*.

To realize that I am no better or worse, no more or less important, than anyone else in the entire world – that only my Awareness is different.

To be different, to make mistakes, to be "wrong," to be inadequate.

To take the time and effort to fulfill *my own* needs.

To be happy and free – to be harmonious and effective – to succeed in every undertaking.

To be open and kind, loving and lovable – compassionate and helpful.

To be keenly sensitive and aware – radiantly healthy and energetic.

To overeat – to indulge my sensual appetites, to lie and to cheat.

To do less than perfect – to be inefficient, to procrastinate, to "goof off," to kill time.

To perceive myself as an absolute "nothing" – unworthy and unneeded.

To have "unacceptable" thoughts, fantasies, desires and experiences.

To allow others to make mistakes, to be "wrong," – to be ignorant, to be "screwed-up."

To be emotional – to love, to cry, to be angry, to hate – to scream, shout and swear – to be selfish and uncaring.

To drop all masks and images – to *not* fulfill others' expectations and images.

To be "closed off," hostile and condemnatory, to be inappropriate.

To let myself be judged – to be hurt, to be anxious, to be fear-ridden.

To feel shame, to blame myself, to experience guilt and remorse.

To use socially unacceptable words and terms – to present a poor image.

To be depressed, tense, impatient and at cross-purposes with myself.

To be generous, to be penurious, to be a spendthrift.

To be lazy, cowardly, disloyal, petty and mean.

To be rich, to be poor – to be selfish, greedy and aggressive.

To be criticized, condemned, disapproved, disliked and unwanted.

To *fail* – to feel "less than," to be despised, rejected and embittered.

To act spontaneously, to resist, to change my mind, to be stubborn.

To be loyal, courageous and *exceptional* – in both my person and my work.

To ACCEPT MY OWN AUTHORITY – TO FOLLOW MY OWN "KNOWING."

BUT, although I allow myself *complete freedom,* I recognize that *I am inescapably responsible* for my *every decision and action.* For I must inevitably pay the price demanded for my actions. I cannot "have my cake and eat it too" for I profit or suffer, learn and grow according to the nature and consequences of my acts. I realize that "good and evil," "right and wrong," are but intellectual concepts, for there is only wisdom and unwisdom, only wise and unwise acts. Therefore prior to a serious decision, I ask myself: "Is this act wise?" i.e., "Will it injure myself or others – will it contribute to my basic needs – is it in alignment with reality – with the laws and forces of life?" What is the *total price involved* and will I be *able* and *willing* to pay it? *Am I willing to accept the consequences?*

I know that in the final analysis I need answer *only to myself* for I profit or suffer accordingly. I know I have all the time there is for my learning and growth – that at worst, I can only postpone my ultimate unfoldment. However, wisdom and love, freedom and joy beckon me onward and *I choose* to proceed as rapidly as my current Awareness permits.

13

Death

When I die, regardless of the manner or situation, I earnestly hope my family and friends will all wish me well and rejoice with me in my new adventure. Life for me is a rich and exciting experience; however, I am absolutely confident that death can only be the opening into something bigger and better. Besides, "everybody is doing it" — it must be all right!

Seriously, though, I love life very much and find it very rich and meaningful, for over the years I have learned to free myself from many erroneous concepts and self-imposed limitations. Actually, I do not believe that anyone can experience this degree of richness and freedom who has a serious reluctance to die, for otherwise one is limited by the very fear of death.

While I have no clear or fixed idea of what is beyond death, I am grateful for the conviction — and it is a conviction of feeling, not of the intellect — that the Power that put me here knows full well when to take me up again; and this in spite of the "accidental" death of my generously endowed only son at age 23.

To believe that there is no directing Power and Purpose — which for want of a better name I call God — is for me harder to disbelieve than to believe as Conklin the noted biologist said, that an explosion in the print shop created Webster's unabridged dictionary. To me death is but the closing of one door and the opening of another. And who are we mortals to assume that the new door will open on something morbid and dread, or to dictate when that door shall open?

I have come to feel that death is a reward that we must earn by serving the living (as in the death of a child) and/or by learning certain necessary lessons through our trials and tribulations while living. Some of us may perhaps have more lessons to learn, or more service than others to perform, before we are permitted to die. The conditions or manner in which we die must also have reason and purpose, even though beyond our human comprehension. We try to see and understand death and "beyond" with our finite, mortal mind which is, of course, impossible since the finite cannot possibly perceive the nature and purpose of the infinite.

As to the question of when we shall die, it is perhaps well to realize that the instant we are born — that very same instant — we are old enough to die. Therefore, we may as well go ahead and make friends with death, for I don't believe we can really make friends with life until we actually accept death as a good and natural part of life. So why not live richly and fully in the *present instant*, freely letting go of the past, which is dead, and with confidence and faith, leave the future to God, in whose hands we have ever been and eternally will be anyway. In any event, we live from the unknown into the known, and from the known into the unknown. Why not, then, through unfailing and careful observation of ourselves and our environment, plus constant self-inquiry, followed by our *own* clear thinking, learn all we possibly can about ourselves and others so that we can live more harmoniously and effectively? If we endeavor to always do the best job of *living* in the *present instant* that we have the wisdom to perceive and the capacity to enjoy, we cannot only *live* in peace but also *die* in peace. For we can then lay down our lives when our individual time comes without reluctance or fear, knowing full well that we have ever done the best we could at the time — and *no man* can do better!

Despite our anxiety and fear, we cannot separate ourselves from our Source, no matter what we may think or how hard we may try. We can only, through a sense of guilt and self-rejection, *feel* that we are separated and then, of course, we suffer accordingly until we find our way back to "our Father's house."

NOTE: The above was written in 1961. Following are excerpts from a letter written to friends immediately after my wife's death from cancer, Christmas Eve, 1970.

..."As you all know, Anne and I have always been extremely close. And for this richly satisfying relationship we have ever been most appreciative. So much so, in fact, that despite Brent's 'tragic' death, our many mistakes and resulting heartaches, and even Anne's recent illness and terrible suffering, we have always considered ourselves the most fortunate — indeed, the most blessed — couple in the world. For we realized that it is the *quality* of life — loving and caring, the meaning and depth of shared friendships and experiences, both happy and sad, the perception and joyful appreciation of life's fabulous gifts — an exhilarating zest for life — rather than the *quantity* of time lived, that constitutes 'good fortune.' And these blessings we enjoyed in overflowing abundance for over forty wonderful years. So we were all reconciled to her passing and had lovingly released her to a new, and I am confident, a much freer and happier existence. Really our only regret was that she and I could not go together. And, thankfully, since neither of us had any fear or dread of death, we had good communication to the very end. We talked freely and easily of her impending death and of my future without her. But even so *(despite her weakness and suffering)* we had some of our most meaningful and deeply happy times during this period.

"Fortunately, we both had a feeling of 'rightness' — a deep conviction that there was meaning and purpose behind her suffering and that it was time for her 'promotion.' For we perceived life as a 'cosmic school room' where everything, especially our suffering, contributes to our needed learning and growth — to an expanded awareness, the only thing we can take with us when we pass into the next stage of our unfoldment. And, believe me, we both did a lot of 'growing' over this last year and a quarter! Actually, I consider Anne 'the lucky one,' for I feel, deep down, that death is the most exciting and wonderful adventure one can possibly experience. Indeed, I look forward to mine with eager anticipation, and *only partly* because of the joyful expectation of once again meeting Anne and Brent, and other loved ones.

"But *my greatest blessing of all* is, that just as happened at our son's death, with whom I was also extremely close, I feel absolutely no sense of grief or loss, for I am so vitally aware of her continuing 'presence,' or possibly 'consciousness' is a better term. Whatever it is, it is very real and wonderful. From the instant I realized she had stopped breathing, I was almost overcome with gratitude for her release from suffering, followed almost immediately by this sense of continuing companionship. Even though I realized I would no longer be seeing her around the house and garden, I had a sense of exhilaration and quiet happiness — the whole place was suddenly alive with her presence and fantastically warm and inviting, even the bedroom where she had just died."

16

ELEMENTS OF FREEDOM

Based on my many years of intensive search and self-discovery, and my resulting high degree of inner peace and rich enjoyment of life, having started from a near "classic" case of self-rejection and disintegrating emotional turmoil, I am absolutely convinced that if life is hurting us, we are not "doing it right." We can resist or try to escape the pain through frenzied activities or destructive self-indulgence, or we can, by isolating the causes, achieve more harmonious growth.

What you are about to read is not speculation or theory. It comes from my own troubled experience — out of my own deep emotional turmoil and hurting, out of corrosive self-rejection and desperate search for meaning, and out of my carefully considered observations in working with others who were suffering.

While I concede that possibly my observations are somewhat distorted and my conclusions perhaps not totally valid, I speak very positively owing to deep convictions arising from the way my findings have revolutionized my life, as well as how dramatically they have affected the lives of others who have incorporated my findings into their living experience.

Just as any physical pain is both a symptom of a physical maladjustment or injury and a warning to take corrective action, so is emotional pain a necessary goad to our learning and growth, to the expansion of our individual consciousness. And until we face up to and come to grips with such pain, we will continue to suffer.

One of man's greatest blessings is inner freedom — the emotional freedom to be one's self regardless of the pressures generated by the values, desires, expectations and attempted control of others. Especially vital is the freedom from the compulsive needs of a crippling lack of self-esteem, of an inadequate sense of self-worth, that requires others' confirmation and agreement — acceptance and approval of others.

Such freedom is truly a "pearl beyond price," for only to the degree that one is inwardly free can he experience the full wonder and richness of life. Only to the degree that he accepts his innate worth and importance in the scheme of things, to the degree that he genuinely loves and cherishes his own precious being, is he free to accept and love his fellowman. For when he denies his own worth and importance, he degrades his self-hood and thus, cannot possibly afford to accept and love others. For this deep, though often unconscious, sense of unworthiness literally forces him to dislike and criticize others in an effort to compensate for his dislike and rejection of himself.

We erroneously believe that others' acceptance and approval of us will automatically insure appreciation and acceptance of ourselves. This fallacious belief is responsible for many of our most destructive motivations. It is, in fact, primarily responsible for roundly condemned selfish striving, fierce ambition and vicious competition, as well as many other distorted drives and actions. (Boastful talk and egocentric action are themselves the strongest proofs of one's lack of self-appreciation and acceptance.)

A person can become extremely successful, enjoy power, prestige and acceptance to his highest expectations and yet have a destructive lack of appreciation of his own personal worth. It is this factor more than any other that binds and prevents us from becoming free. It drives us unmercifully to compete fiercely and aggressively, with little or no concern for others. We become so involved with our own real and fancied inadequacies that we are either unaware of others' needs and problems, or feel unable to *afford* the time and attention to concern ourselves with them.

Only when you are free to feel warm and friendly toward yourself can you give and receive love. And only to such degree can you relate with others on a deeply meaningful level. If one genuinely loves himself, and gratefully accepts his intrinsic worth and importance, he automatically foregoes greed, hostility, envy and aggression, for he no longer experiences the sense of inadequacy and dependence that generate such emotions. In fact, if man were inwardly free — free of the anxiety, hate and aggression inherent in one with an inadequate sense of self-worth — he would no longer experience the inner turmoil and violence that externalize as a need for outer violence and killing. He would then, in fact, be incapable of hating and murdering his fellowman. The *seeds* of war — the hate, greed, aggression, and the drive to be "better than" and the compulsive need for exorbitant power and prestige — could no longer find fertile ground in which to grow and flourish.

The fundamental truth, although rarely recognized, is that we are *inherently* free. The choice is *always ours.* We have the freedom to choose absolutely anything we want — anything at all. Our only limitation to actualizing this freedom harmoniously and effectively is our limited perception which may not recognize this freedom, and our limited wisdom which does not always allow us to choose wisely and well.

Nevertheless, we are *potentially* free to choose anything we want, including selfishness, violence, murder, rape, incest, love, sharing, self-denial, dependence, independence, money, penury, extravagance, work, idleness, self-indulgence, or whatever. *The choice is always ours* even though the foreseeable consequences of our decisions and actions often make us lose sight of our *potential* freedom. This is because we are often unwilling to even face the *possibilities* of such consequences.

Although not subject to blame, we are totally *responsible* for our every act inasmuch as the inexorable law of cause and effect will not permit us to escape the consequences we set in motion, be they good or bad. Thus, we profit or suffer accordingly, as well as often involving others, to either their benefit or detriment. It is primarily owing to the consequences of our *mistakes*, however, that we learn and grow. They not only show us how to do better "next time" but also how to function more effectively in completely new situations.

The potential consequences of our actions determine the price demanded for every decision. Inner freedom is dependent on a clear perception of both the potential benefits and the total price involved. The coin may be in effort, money, physical and emotional energy, emotional turmoil, anxiety and hurt, physical pain and suffering. Or it may be in foregoing the possible benefits of one alternative for another, the denial of a given need or desire for a cherished moral value, or of another meaningful need unsuccessfully competing for fulfillment.

Careful observation of both our own acts and those of others, plus honest and searching inquiry into our reasons for so doing, will disclose three fundamental, as well as crucially important actualities:

1.   Every human act is a conscious or unconscious response to a personal need, emotional or otherwise.

2.   We do *only* that which we are motivated to do — that which *we would rather do than not do*. Thus, if we wish to deliberately improve our individual conduct — or that of society, since society is but a collection of individuals — it is essential that we understand both the motivation and the need which generated it. It is also important to realize that, despite appearances to the contrary and even though it may adversely affect us, seldom is another's action truly *personal to us*. Our involvement in the act is normally only incidental in the expression of the other's need. We but intercept "the arrow" dispatched toward the nearest available target by one's emotional hurt, anger or frustration — by his compelling need of the instant.

3.   The nature of one's motivation, whether destructive or constructive, murderous or altruistic, depends on one's individual stage of consciousness, his degree of perception and wisdom.

Regardless of the various factors going into the formation of one's motivation, he invariably chooses only that alternative which he *wants more* than any other, that which *he would rather do than not do*. For we do absolutely nothing *without sufficient motivation* — whether the decision is to get up out of a chair or to put ourselves through college. Even such things as self-discipline, bravery, cowardice, ambition, laziness, industry and thrift, are but expressions of our *dominant motivation,* conscious or unconscious, at a particular time. Actually, everyone is motivated, even though his motivation may be simply to sit and dream his life away. Thus, the only possible way a person can be changed is through a *change in his motivation,* which normally involves a change in one's needs or his perception of his needs.

An improved motivation *cannot,* however, *be achieved on demand.* It can only come into being through one's increased *Awareness and understanding,* a clearer perception and more intelligent evaluation of all the pros and cons. Recognition of this basic truth points the way to all constructive human effort, and hopefully will dispel much of our current wishful, unreal, hurtful thinking, as well as our futile and destructive moralizing.

Our problems of anti-social behavior can be resolved only through *individual realization* of the *actualities of human conduct — a realization* of how and why we function as we do in order to achieve the understanding and thereby generate the motivation necessary to live more harmoniously and effectively.

So-called "will power," for example, is actually nothing more nor less than the power generated by focusing of our desire. *Absolutely nothing* was ever accomplished by a *"sheer act of will."* This concept is a complete fallacy, for we *never do anything* except take care of our individual dominant need and *desire of the instant.* We *exercise* this so-called "will power" simply by generating or intensifying our *motivation* through *mentally imaging* the potential benefits expected to accrue from *doing* or *not doing* the thing in question. Conversely, a "weak-willed" person is simply one who does not have, or is unable to, generate *sufficient motivation* for a proposed action. A peaceful person is one who senses his primary needs and desires sufficiently clearly and imaginatively to generate more than simply enough motivation to grudgingly act as he feels he *"should."* Such a one is so aware of the potential benefits that he is *completely* convinced they are well worth, or *more than worth*, the price demanded. He is thus free of disintegrating conflict, doubt, confusion, fear and indecision — basic handicaps to one's inherently high spirits, inner freedom and peace of mind.

Procrastination, on the other hand, results from insufficient motivation to overcome inertia, competing needs or fear of failure. To eliminate it we need but make a careful evaluation of potential benefits versus the adverse effects of inaction and decide accordingly.

Effective self-discipline is, itself, but one's ability to generate sufficient motivation to do what conforms with his individual values and aspirations. Thus, without well-defined values and aspirations, effective self-discipline is impossible.

Ideally, in decision-making our prevailing perception and wisdom intelligently weigh the potential benefits of the various alternatives against their corresponding consequences so as to determine (1) the *total* price demanded, (2) whether or not we can *afford* such price, and (3) whether we are *willing* to pay it.

Unfortunately, our prevailing understanding does not always allow us to accurately determine the above three factors, in which case we not only make an unwise decision but confusion, conflict and frustration result from our inability to make a clear-cut satisfying choice between our competing needs and desires. For instance, owing to our individual system of values, we often reluctantly give up a strong desire in order to honor a somewhat stronger moral value, not realizing that we *are* doing what we *most* want to do.

The following six factors determine our dominant motivation *at any given time*, as well as how deliberately and objectively we are able to weigh available alternatives. Having once achieved definite motivation, our decision and action are relatively straight-forward. The establishment of a specific motivation, however, is itself sometimes quite puzzling since the origin or basis of such motivation is often difficult to determine because of unrecognized instinctual drives and hidden urges.

These six factors are:

1. Inner drives stemming from instinctive, subconscious or intuitive urges of which we may not be aware.

2. The impact of environmental pressures generated by our material needs for food, clothing and shelter, as well as our emotional need for a sense of security and belonging, identity, self-expression, love. These latter so-called "ego-needs" may make us desperate for the confirmation and approval of others — so much so, in fact, that until we find our own identity and authority we are compulsive *"people pleasers."* This is not only terribly destructive to our self-esteem, for it is, in effect, a denial of our very self-hood, but it also makes us feel extremely vulnerable to others' reactions since we are so emotionally dependent on their approval and acceptance.

3. Prevailing emotions such as depression, fear, hate, hostility, resentment, anger, envy, jealousy, love, joy and exuberance.

4. Our total conditioning — our learned knowledge, desires, values, concepts, prejudices, beliefs, assumptions, habits, etc.

5. Our intellectual ability to think clearly and logically — to correlate and evaluate with relevance and accuracy.

6. Our reservoir of emotional and physical energy. This will dictate an alternative choice in case we cannot afford the energy necessary for an otherwise preferred option.

An absolutely fundamental fact, the recognition of which is crucially important to our effective and harmonious functioning, is that these six factors, plus our prevailing perception and wisdom, which monitor and ultimately allow our decisions, are absolutely *fixed* or *frozen* at the *instant of decision* just as the legs of a racing horse are "stopped" by a high speed camera. With this fact in mind, it is self-evident that *everyone invariably* makes the *only* choice he possibly can at any particular instant, regardless of how undesirable or hurtful the resulting consequences may be to himself or others. How could it possibly be otherwise, all factors considered? Somewhat later, of course, one may make an entirely different choice, based on new insight or data obtained from the consequences of his previous choice — or perhaps because of a change in another of the above factors. However, at the time in question, his prevailing understanding automatically, consciously or unconsciously, integrated these factors as they actually existed *at the time* — and inevitably came up with the *only* answer *then* possible. Thus, his choice, however good or bad, moral or immoral, wise or unwise, was absolutely the *very best* he was *capable* of making at that *particular instant* like it or not. What other conclusion can one logically make?

To summarize, one always does *only* what he is *motivated* to do. And the various factors which *determine* one's dominant motivation are fixed or frozen at the instant of his every decision. Thus, one invariably does the *only thing*, and therefore the *best thing*, of which he is capable at the time, all pertinent factors considered.

A further vitally important fact apparent in this analysis of the *reality of decision-making* is that neither adulation, pride nor condemnation are ever valid reactions. Acknowledgment of merit or error, self-satisfaction, pleasure or displeasure, gratification or disappointment, approval or disapproval, appreciation or dislike, YES; but NEVER are either credit or condemnation rationally *justifiable*. Not credit, for one can do only that which his current capabilities, understanding and motivation impel him to do. *He cannot do otherwise.* He could not posssibly change any of these factors without the necessary understanding and motivation to do so. Likewise, condemnation is never justified, for again, since he could not possibly do otherwise, all factors considered, he did the best he possibly could at the time. And *who* can do better than his *best*? Furthermore, and for the same reasons, how can we possibly justify *punishment*, other than as a corrective or restraining measure? And what of *capital punishment*? Of revenge?

In light of this, is not man's character no more than an aggregate of his dominant motivations — none of which he can change or direct on demand?

Our freedom lies in the fact that we *always* have the option to increase our understanding and thereby achieve improved motivation for the future, *provided*, of course, that we can be so motivated, or ourselves generate the necessary motivation to do so.

From the foregoing, it is a self-evident fact that there is absolutely no justification for shame, blame, guilt or remorse, even though we *are* inevitably *responsible* for our every choice and act. Regret, to the degree determined by the gravity of the adverse consequences — a sincere desire that we had done better — is natural and constructive, as long as it contains no self-condemnation or guilt. Such regret is actually helpful in inducing us to act more wisely in the future.

This recognition of the reality of our individual freedom is a *profound concept*, for it not only presents conclusive and rational proof that we are never justifiably subject to inhibiting and destructive blame and guilt for past actions, but it also shows that our future is ever wide open for improvement. For we can, if sufficiently motivated, always do better through deliberately increasing our understanding of the various factors affecting our lives. We *can* thereby learn to function more harmoniously and effectively. And if the conditions prevailing in our lives *do not* fully meet our expectations and desires, it is definitely up to us to do something about them — not the government, society or "Uncle John." For the *choice is always ours!*

We inevitably get what we *earn* through our own choice — be it good or bad. The law of compensation, though seldom as apparent or quick in its operation, is just as inexorable as the law of gravity. Other people and their acts are but *instrumental* in our growth and development — in our success or failure.

It can be readily seen from this analysis of decision-making that to label our acts "right" or "wrong," "good" or "bad," in a moral sense, is completely invalid, totally without logical support. Moral declarations are never justified except for *describing* wise or unwise acts. For there is only *wisdom* and *unwisdom*! Unexamined moral values, even if sound and well-founded in their inception, can be no more than arbitrary guides to harmonious and constructive conduct — substitutes for the spontaneous direction of one's innate perception and wisdom.

Moral *admonitions*, moreover, are often *destructive*, for they cause only resistance, guilt and resentment in the one who does not have the required understanding and *motivation*

22

to comply with them. Incidentally, they are often urged by one who is, himself, unable to comply with them.

Only when we deliberately and completely drop our framework of "right and wrong," "good and evil," and simply evaluate acts as wise or unwise, are we sufficiently *free* to perceive and enjoy the full richness and beauty of life as it *actually is.* In addition to generating the totally destructive emotions of shame, blame, guilt and remorse, condemnation and moral admonitions often cause one to *live* as he is *labeled,* that is, a liar, thief, or moral leper, as the case may be. For he feels constrained to live up to his reputation no matter how bad it may be.

The master key for effective living is a *sound self-concept,* a conscious appreciation of our individual worth and importance, that derives from recognition of one's innate value and uniqueness, one's genuine self-acceptance and warm regard for his own *precious being.* It cannot be gained by comparing one's achievements and possessions with those of others.

This essential characteristic can be best achieved through adequate self-understanding. Such understanding can be most readily accomplished by a conscientious program of self-discovery — careful observation and self-inquiry into the values, needs, urges, motivations and actions of both ourselves and others. Another prime requisite is to acknowledge our *own* authority and assume *full* responsibility — take complete charge of our individual lives and direct them as we, ourselves, see fit. We are free to do *anything we desire.* It is, however, highly advisable that we first try to ascertain the total price, that we can *afford* such price, and finally, that we are *willing* to pay it despite unknown risks.

It is no wonder that our society is sick, "well nigh unto death," as witnessed by our brutalities, rank hypocrisy, racial strife, emotional turmoil, poverty and deprivation, the rebellion of our youth and the acceptance of legalized murder as a means of resolving international quarrels. For lack of self-appreciation, our self-rejection and self-hate are practically a universal problem, largely fostered by the totally erroneous principle of *glorification and condemnation,* of *"reward and punishment"* instead of recognition that we are each unique and precious, *invariably* doing our *absolute best* at any given time, all learning and growing, regardless of our mistaken and destructive acts.

It is evident from the foregoing that the solution to our human predicament is totally dependent on increasing our *individual* perception and wisdom and thereby our genuine *acceptance of self.* For there are no mass remedies or quick and easy cures. Intellectualizing alone can never furnish an effective answer.

The grim truth is that it is patently impossible for us to function as a free and peaceful society until we are inwardly free and at peace with ourselves. Just as surely as night follows day, our inner turmoil and violence, our self-rejection and hate, our distorted perceptions and values cannot but objectify in our overt acts and attitudes throughout our environment. There can be no external peace and freedom without inner peace and freedom! And inner peace and freedom can only become a reality through self-understanding and self-acceptance. We can achieve full self-acceptance only when we take full responsibility for our own lives and stop trying to make ourselves "right" by condemning others; when we encourage autonomy rather than inflicting needless control; when we recognize the fact that we are each unique and precious — no one innately better or worse, and in an ultimate sense, no one more or less important than another — each responsible for his own learning and growth; each a part of the same cosmic unity. Only then comes the realization that "when you hurt, I hurt." Only when these basic requirements are met can we fully experience a genuine sense of self-worth, freedom, peace and love — love of both ourselves and for one another. And only then can we live in peace and harmony, one with another!

THE CHOICE IS OURS

In an ultimate sense, *every* decision we make is *voluntary*. This fundamental fact is often denied or overlooked because the price of the only perceivable alternative is so exorbitant that we do not recognize our option or refuse to consider it. For example, a thief demands our money or our life, and without even considering giving up our life, we hurriedly hand over our pocketbook. Even though this choice may appear ridiculously obvious, the fact is that *we are* inherently free to make *any choice we wish.*

Recognition of this reality is crucially important to our general well-being, for it precludes much emotional resistance, resentment and often rebellion. The absence or significant reduction of such inner tensions permits contact with our inner wisdom as well as allowing us to see possible alternatives more clearly and to consider them more calmly and intelligently. Consequently, we function more effectively and harmoniously, for we profit or suffer according to the wisdom of our every choice.

Realization that the choice is always *ours* and recognition of how our choices are determined are vital to a thorough understanding of the terms "free will," "will power," "sheer act of will," "strength of character," "self-discipline," "motivation," etc. And it is only through a complete understanding of these terms that we can free ourselves to act more honestly and realistically — and still more to the point, more intentionally and constructively determine our own lives.

While we are free to make any decision *we choose,* there is a *price exacted* for *every decision* we make, for in making a given decision, we automatically forego all the available alternatives. For example, if I decide to work in my garden on a Sunday afternoon, I must forego reading a favorite book, watching a television program, taking a drive, visiting with friends, etc. And if I am careless in making my decision or don't have all the pertinent facts, I am liable to regret my choice. I may even load myself with blame and guilt, for, say, "selfishly" choosing to care for my garden instead of visiting a sick friend or relative.

But regardless of possible subsequent regret, pain or guilt, I *invariably* did the particular thing I was *motivated* to do — the one thing, all factors considered, I most *wanted* to do at the time (that is, that which I would rather do than not do). And the only way I can change my direction or conduct is through a *change in my motivation!*

This desire or *motivation* to do a specific thing has been labeled "will power." Down through the ages it has been loaded with mystery and worshipped as something very special when it has led to *constructive* acts. On the other hand, when it has led to negative or *socially unacceptable* acts, the doer is at best called "weak-willed" or "willful" and written off as a person of "weak character" — or, depending on the specific act, a degenerate or evil person.

In actual fact, the crucial difference between two of comparable talents is their awareness and specific desire or *motivation.* One may have the conditioned values and understanding to act constructively, or perhaps have been fired with a burning desire to accomplish a great engineering feat or work of art. Whereas the other may not have had the values or the understanding to *pay the required price for a wise action,* or he may even, owing to real or fancied injustice and the resulting emotional hurt and resentment, be motivated to act rebelliously and destructively.

The fault, if any, for an unwise choice is not in the *person* but in his *erroneous training, lack of understanding,* and/or *emotional hurting.* And until we and people in power understand this and act accordingly, how are we to create a better society, let alone function more harmoniously as individuals? Here we might well reflect on the fact that it has not been too terribly long since debtors were imprisoned — a poignant example of the self-defeating choice of employing punishment and force rather than providing a solution based on an adequate *understanding* of the relevant factors.

As a matter of observable fact, *every decision* we make is the result of our dominant motivation at that particular instant. This motivation in turn is determined by our needs and conditioned values, both conscious and unconscious, interacting with our emotions and the prevailing pressures and circumstances. These values, themselves, are a manifestation of our individual degree of perception and wisdom. A saint, for example, is a saint because his values cause him to *want* to be "good." A thief steals because he wants money or the power of money and has no strong value against stealing. He may even admire the cleverness of an expert thief and want to emulate him. A lazy person is simply one who has not been sufficiently sold on the benefits of working over "getting by" without working. A brave or courageous person is one whose values demand that he do what he does in spite of possible injury or death — his need to act outweighs all foreseeable adverse consequences. He might, for instance, have such an intense value against being considered a coward that he cannot tolerate the possibility of anyone, especially himself, thinking he is lacking in courage. An extremely selfish or self-centered person is simply one whose immediate personal needs are so intense he cannot tolerate their postponement or denial, even at the expense of the needs and desires of others.

Once we accept and understand these principles, we *can* generate *more constructive motivation,* both in ourselves and in others. All such motivation, however, can come only from *increased understanding.* It *cannot* be *supplied on demand* simply because we feel we *"ought"* or *"must"* act more constructively.

Thus, what we treasure in ourselves as "will power" and "strength of character" is but a strong desire or motivation to achieve our individual needs or honor our own particular set of values — to do as we ourselves have been conditioned to do, which may or may not be desirable for others or society as a whole.

A "sheer act of will" is but one's ability to generate a sufficiently intense desire, that is, *motivation,* to accomplish a given objective in spite of serious, sometimes almost overwhelming obstacles. While "will power" itself is but the power generated by *focusing our desires* — conjuring up in our minds all possible benefits to be gained by the proposed act.

By the same token, "self-discipline" can come about only when one has aspirations or goals *sufficiently strong to pay the price demanded.* Naturally, the more immediate and readily appreciated the benefits, the easier it is to generate the required motivation. Likewise, the more distant and questionable the advantages the more difficult it is to achieve the necessary motivation for a given act or conduct. For instance, it is much more difficult to motivate a youngster to save his earnings for a life insurance policy than for a new bike. One is, however, *always* motivated — and at the mercy of his dominant motivation — even though it may be *to do absolutely nothing.*

For example, if I am to stop overeating, I must become "sold" that an agile healthy body, fit appearance, and a sense of victorious self-control are sufficiently desirable to forego self-indulgence in tempting foods as compensation for unfulfilled emotional needs and tensions. I can *never* stop simply because I think I *"should,"* for this only generates self-defeating resistance.

Motivation depends on many and sometimes very complex and even unconscious factors. But the predominant factor required for "right," that is, *wise*, motivation is the perception and wisdom that can only come through discovering how and why we function as we do. We need, therefore, to make a persistent and conscientious effort toward self-discovery and to learn from the adverse consequences of our mistakes. But although we may carefully observe and question our every decision and action, we will not learn much until we stop *condemning* ourselves for our unwise actions. The pain and discomfort resulting from our self-recrimination, shame and guilt force us unconsciously to alibi, rationalize and justify. This defense mechanism makes it impossible to determine the pertinent factors behind our distorted and mistaken actions.

If we will forego all self-condemnation and blame, however, we can learn a great deal about ourselves. For we will then be freed to honestly and realistically evaluate our *motives* by careful observation and investigation of our actions and reactions, our concepts and values, our prejudices, beliefs and assumptions, our moods and attitudes. In the process we will find "right" things done for the "wrong" reasons; for instance, fear of punishment as a motive rather than being sold on the potential benefits of the particular action. We will also find non-constructive things done for *"right"* motives but distorted through a lack of understanding; for example, the destroying of livestock during the depression of the thirties in order to maintain an adequate price for the farmer.

In addition to intellectually checking our motives and their contributing factors, we each possess an intuitive "knowing" that can guide us in determining their source and validity when we are sufficiently free of emotional "static" to tune it in. We must first, of course, discover and encourage this inner spring of wisdom.

Only to the degree that we can control our motivation can we take charge of and direct our own lives. The best means of *consciously generating motivation* is to marshal all the *potential benefits* of a proposed action against the pertinent *negative factors*. We may thereby thoroughly convince ourselves that the proposed act is *well worth* the price demanded. Such a price may be measured in time, effort, money, nervous energy, emotional involvement, real or fancied loss of prestige, or numerous other intangibles. The problem is first to anticipate the total price of a proposed action realistically and then to determine if we are *willing* and *able* to pay it.

Our motivation may stem from others' values and control — from a desire to meet *their* expectations and conform to their demands, rather than to honor *our own*. Until a person recognizes, accepts and exercises his *own* innate wisdom and *authority* and determines his *own* values, however, he cannot be free to be *himself*. And if we are not authentic — not true to our own values and convictions — we will be unable to achieve the sense of self-worth *essential* to our effectivity and well-being.

But until we thoroughly understand that we act *only* through motivation (and not some mythical "will power"), and that with sufficient understanding, *constructive motivation can be generated*, we will continue to damn and devalue both ourselves and our fellowmen for not having sufficient "will power" — not realizing that will power is but a synonym for desire or "desire power." A good example is found in the heavy smoker who continually condemns himself for being "weak-willed" because he is unable to stop in spite of the threat of lung cancer. *Actually,* he has such strong *"will power"* to *smoke* that he is unable to resist the urge. Is this not the same "will power" that enables another, who is so motivated, to *stop* smoking?

The old adage, "where there is a will (that is, motivation), there is a way," is a self-evident fact. We have no doubt each demonstrated more than once in our lives that if we have a *sufficiently intense desire* we almost surely will find a "way," regardless of seemingly impossible obstacles. The relevant point here is that when once we realize that "will" is no more nor less than simply motivation, we *can* then go about *generating it* rather than naively considering it a "gift of the gods" bestowed on a favored few but which we ourselves can do little about.

Moreover, we will also then realize how futile and foolish it is to condemn ourselves or others for not having enough "will power" for certain desirable action or conduct.

All motivation boils down to *whether or not we are willing* to pay the *price required* for a given objective. But we do not operate in a vacuum. We invariably have competing needs and desires, often beyond our conscious ability to control. And one may have to suffer the "tortures of the damned" before he is able to achieve sufficient motivation to do or to forego something essential to his well-being; for instance, witness the plight of the alcoholic or drug addict. I myself have more than once undergone truly agonizing migraine headaches before I was able, that is, *willing,* to forego indulging my taste for chocolate and peanut butter, which among other things, triggered this awful pain. I somehow felt that "this *one* time" I could escape paying the price, in spite of repeated evidence to the contrary.

Making mistakes is, however, the primary way we learn and grow — a way we exercise and profit from our freedom of choice. And while, *potentially,* we can almost always *do better* "next time," the essential ingredient for *actually* doing it is adequate motivation *at the time.* This can be readily verified in our own experience, if we will but honestly consider all pertinent factors, including our conditioned ideas, values, concepts and beliefs. We will inevitably find that *no one* does *anything* that he is not *motivated* to do, regardless of theory or folklore to the contrary.

Although individual patterns of growth may involve greater handicaps and suffering for one than another, we *are* each *responsible* for our own lives and how we live them. And it isn't so much *what happens to us* as *how we handle it* that contributes to our learning and development. Two things, however, are "for sure." First, we can find no real peace or happiness — only confusion, frustration, emotional turmoil and defeat — until we *deliberately take charge of our own lives;* for otherwise we can achieve no genuine sense of self-worth. Secondly, we can effectively deal with things *only* as they actually ARE, *here and now* — NOT as they "should be" or as we *wish* them to be. Wishful thinking can only lead to self-pity, futility and defeat, for it is impossible to cope with unreality! Regardless of handicaps and difficult situations, we must always start from *where we are.* Where we would *like to be* is completely irrelevant to the *immediate* situation. And one thing more — no matter how capable or successful another may be, he cannot possibly make *us* any *"less."* Likewise, how mean or "worthless" others may be cannot possibly make *us* any *"better."* For we each *rise* or *fall* on our *own* individual decisions and efforts. We can only be "better" through achieving *"better" motivation.*

Our individual motivation inexorably determines our every action. We can generate effective and harmonious motivation through increased understanding and thoughtful evaluation. Or we can simply *react* to unconscious urges and outer stimuli and thus unknowingly let happenstance and emotions control and direct our lives. The fundamental problem of humanity is the generation of wise motivation and the full realization that we are each inescapably *responsible* for our every decision and act.

We CAN and DO *determine the course of our lives.* Are we going to do it unknowingly and by default — or are we *deliberately* and *knowingly* going to opt for happiness and peace of mind? THE CHOICE IS OURS!

11-1-69   L.S. Barksdale

FRIENDSHIP

Friends are people who are drawn together in undemanding companionship by an intangible affinity and mutually shared interests and personal concerns.

Who have deep affection, respect, and admiration for each other, free from any taint of possessiveness or trace of competition; who, regardless of external appearances, prestige or possessions, accept each other as equals on an equal basis.

Who recognize and accept each other's weaknesses and lacks as well as their strengths and blessings with the full realization that each is as God made him — each pursuing his individual path toward self-knowledge and freedom, even though he may often stumble and slip backward in his upward struggle.

Who drop all masks and are completely open and sincere with each other — not bound or influenced by petty conventions and artificial social values and usages.

Who both receive and give without the slightest sense of obligation. Who ever extend moral support and warm understanding — and who can share their inmost treasures, free of all reservations and without fear of being considered "less" for so doing.

Who are both willing and free to allow each other their own values and to be mutually vulnerable — and who rejoice in the freedom of such a relationship; knowing without question, that the other is a rock of faith and deep understanding — one with whom he can unabashedly lick his wounds of hostile human encounters.

Who rejoice in the growth and well-being of each other and with glowing satisfaction and thankful happiness are ever aware, "you are my friend."

This is, of course, whether or not we realize it, the kind of relationship we are all seeking, particularly with wife or husband. And it is the kind of relationship we must encourage and develop between parent and child if each is to be free and independent — and thus an emotionally healthy individual.

Lilburn S. Barksdale

31

KEY TO FRIENDSHIP

Ideally, friends are people who are drawn together in undemanding companionship by an intangible affinity and mutually shared interests and personal concerns. Who have deep affection, respect, and admiration for each other, free from any taint of possessiveness, envy, or striving to be "better than." Who, regardless of external appearances, prestige or possessions, accept each other as equals on an equal basis.

Who recognize and accept each other's weaknesses and lacks as well as their strengths and blessings with the full realization that each is a manifestation of his current state of Awareness — each pursuing his individual path toward greater perception and wisdom, even though he may often stumble and slip backward in his upward struggle.

Who drop all masks and are completely open and sincere with each other — not bound or influenced by petty conventions and artificial social values and usages. Who both receive and give without the slightest sense of obligation. Who ever extend moral support and warm understanding — and who can share their inmost treasures, free of all reservations and without fear of being considered "less" for so doing.

Who are free to allow each other their own values, beliefs and opinions — and who rejoice in the freedom of such a relationship, knowing, without question, that the other is a rock of faith and deep understanding — one with whom he can unabashedly lick the wounds of hostile human encounters. Who rejoice in the growth and well-being of each other and with glowing satisfaction and thankful happiness, are ever aware, "you are my friend."

This is, of course, the kind of relationship we are all seeking, particularly with wife or husband. And it is the kind of relationship we must encourage and develop between parent and child if each is to be free and independent — and thus an emotionally healthy individual. It is, however, impossible to achieve until we stop demanding the other be something he isn't, or do something his Awareness does not permit.

Every man is a manifestation of his current state of Awareness. A newborn baby is aware of light and darkness, the surrounding temperatures, a need to nurse, fearful when his hunger is not quickly satisfied. He is afraid of falling and soon becomes aware that when he cries he will receive attention — that when he laughs and gurgles people can scarcely resist his overtures. At some point he realizes that those enticing toes waving around near the foot of the crib are actually a part of him, to be played with as he chooses. And so on and on, he continually becomes more and more aware of himself and of his environment. Eventually he learns that certain acts cause physical pain and others emotional hurt. He becomes quite thoroughly *conditioned* to his environment and to the moral and social values of his group — to know what is expected of him and to conform or rebel as he elects.

His perception and understanding are limited or expanded, modified or distorted by many and often complex factors. He reacts to his inner drives and urges — his ego drive for self-expression and acceptance — to the adverse or beneficial consequences of his every choice; to the prevailing mores, concepts, and personalities of his group; and to the events and pressures of his environment. But at any given instant, like it or not, our individual Awareness, "good" or "bad" as the case may be, *is what it IS.*

Our *every* thought, act and reaction, our concepts, attitudes, beliefs and values, our every motivation, are but symptoms of our individual perception and wisdom. Clear or distorted, our perception sadly limited or enlightened as the case may be, *we are what we are* at any given time — and think, act and react accordingly. For all the factors which determine our thoughts and current behavior are fixed or frozen at the instant of our every reaction and decision.

This is a fundamental fact of life, the recognition and acceptance of which is essential for our emotional freedom, tranquility and enduring happiness. We can criticize, condemn and denounce another for his lack of wisdom or consideration, his dishonesty, cowardice or "moral degradation," for his foolish or hurtful acts, his appearance and style of living, his anti-social attitude and selfish behavior — but all to no avail. For whether or not our criticism or demands are justified, one can only do what his *prevailing* Awareness dictates. And he can only *change* through *a change in his Awareness.*

This does not mean that we should condone or passively accept hurtful or anti-social acts. But it points the way to dealing with them constructively. Until we recognize this underlying fact and accept and understand it deep within our consciousness, we will continue to resist and resent, to find fault, to blame, condemn and denounce. Likewise, we will experience shame, blame, guilt and remorse within ourselves. And we will be unable to experience inner freedom, open and loving relationships, peace, happiness and joy until we do *stop criticizing and condemning one another.* Otherwise, we are caught up in destructive emotions, mental blocks and defeating tensions. Thus, while it is essential to our optimum learning and growth to observe, analyze and carefully evaluate puzzling situations and the behavior of others, condemnation and denunciation prevent us from being objective, emotionally free and happy. For condemnation causes hostility and resentment, expressed or repressed, for all concerned.

It is only through an increased Awareness that we can see beyond the world of effects and symptoms to the *causes* of our dilemmas and problems. And we cannot fully resolve them until we do. With greater perception and wisdom can we improve our motivation and thereby act more wisely and harmoniously. However, we cannot deliberately better our understanding and motivation until we *first* have a sufficiently strong desire to do so. Such motivation, itself, can stem only from an awareness of such need and the potential rewards of its fulfillment. It cannot be supplied on demand simply because of the values and desires of society or of another person — from their "oughts," "shoulds" and "musts." We can do a thing only when we are *sold*, consciously or unconsciously, on its accomplishment being worth the *price* we must pay, whether in money, time, effort, self-denial, hurt to our ego, etc. — only when, all things considered, we would rather do that particular thing than not do it.

Only through an open, non-judgmental attitude, fostered by the realization that our every act is dictated by our current Awareness, can we achieve a free, rich and rewarding relationship with members of our family, with our co-workers, in fact, with anyone we meet. Only then can we recognize and appreciate the real person behind his mask and actions, his appearance and personality.

We can manage such a relationship, however, only to the degree that we accept and feel warm and loving toward *ourselves.* For we cannot *afford* to be kind, gentle and loving toward others when we are so tied up in our own real and fancied inadequacies and self-rejection. We cannot feel really good toward ourselves until we stop all self-recrimination, repudiate all shame and guilt, and take *complete* charge of our individual lives — until we recognize and *exercise* our innate authority — until we *deliberately* and *habitually* choose the particular alternative that looks the best to *us*, not to some authority figure or someone we want to please at the expense of our own integrity. And we must also stop blaming other people and conditions for our inadequacies, problems and mistakes. For when we do so we unconsciously deny and devalue our own worth — we do not perceive ourselves as whole and independent persons who are capable of taking complete responsibility for our own lives.

Also, owing to our human frailties, mistakes, personal defeats and sense of inadequacy, it is practically impossible to accept and love ourselves until we realize, deep within our consciousness, *who we are* — that we are essentially *non-physical beings* — infinitely more than just a body and ego intellect stumbling around in search of self-approval and acceptance — of a sense of meaning and personal importance. We did not just *happen* any more than a book happens because of an explosion in the print shop.

To be able to extend genuine friendship, we must be free and at peace with ourselves; we must accept and play the cards the way they are dealt, regardless of how "unfair," distasteful or painful this may be. We need realize, however, that we can *be responsible* only for those things which we, ourselves, can *affect or change*. It is not *our problem* if there is nothing constructive *we* can *do about* a situation.

We each have our individual pattern of unfoldment — our "own way to go." Every experience is a needed lesson in our learning and growth, in the expansion of our Awareness. It is evident that some of us have a much harder way to go than others. We can be sure, however, that every experience, no matter how distasteful or painful, has meaning and purpose. Our individual growth *can be* very painful, but despite any appearances to the contrary, we do not live in a world of chaos and happenstance. The sky does not fall or the sun fail to rise. Joy and love *can be* experienced when we obtain a sufficient degree of Awareness.

But we can only deal successfully with things as they ARE. Our responsibility is simply to do the best we can under the prevailing conditions and circumstances, beginning HERE and NOW!

Wringing our hands and worrying about things we can do nothing about is both injurious to our effectivity and our opinion of ourselves, plus a sad waste of time and energy. We can best help both ourselves and our friends through expanding our own Awareness by observing, analyzing and honestly evaluating our personal concepts, assumptions, beliefs, and values — by carefully investigating our attitudes, *motives* and emotional reactions. We cannot give a thirsting brother a drink from an empty jug.

1-2-70   L.S. Barksdale

I BELIEVE

That "sin" is but a synonym for "mistake," and "evil" but a descriptive term for the effects of unwise decisions and actions. That *all* "evil" springs from our limited awareness and the resulting distortion of our needs.

That we can do only what we are *motivated* to do, i.e., that which we *most* want to do — that which we would rather do than not do.

That everyone invariably does the best he can at the time, for his motivation is determined at any given instant by his prevailing awareness and active needs, conscious and unconscious, instinctive and intuitive.

That our motivation, and therefore our choice, is inevitably dictated by our current awareness and needs, however limited or distorted they may be at the time.

That the only way we can possibly do better is through "better" motivation and that this can come from, and only from, greater awareness, regardless of the source of our knowledge and insights.

That to *"know better,"* in the sense of "right" values, is not sufficient to *"do better"* if the intensity of our prevailing need is greater than that of the value in question.

That, therefore, at any given instant we *each* invariably do *what we have to do*, despite the negative or destructive consequences of our choice or action.

That "moral action" is but descriptive of acts generally agreed on as acceptable by a particular group or culture.

That unless moral values are understood to be simply *guides* to desirable conduct for the less aware, they generate inhibiting and destructive self-condemnation, shame, blame, guilt and remorse in those unable, because of intense conflicting needs, to comply with such values.

That the only sound motivation for "right" — that is, "wise" — action is a clear understanding of both the benefits and the total price, that is, the full consequences incurred by the proposed decision or action.

That we are each *inevitably responsible* for our every act, for whether or not we are aware of the fact, we cannot possibly escape paying the total price demanded — we invariably benefit or suffer depending on the wisdom or unwisdom of our acts, regardless of whether or not we can anticipate and are willing to accept the total consequences.

That the meaning and purpose of life is *learning and growth*, for an expanded awareness is the *only thing* we can take with us when we "die."

MY REALITY
(A Personal Reminder and Guide)

My "Awareness" is the degree that I *perceive* and *understand* everything that affects my life.

I, myself, *am fully responsible* for both my material and emotional well-being. There is always a way out of my troubles if I will but focus my Awareness and search it out. My problems are as big as my futile worry and brooding make them.

Despite all personal handicaps and environmental pressures — regardless of my faulty conditioning and limited Awareness — I profit or suffer according to the *wisdom* or *unwisdom* of my every act, conscious or non-conscious. Thus, I cannot possibly escape responsibility for my decisions.

The basic law of the universe is: "As ye sow, so shall ye reap." Lack of Awareness and the resulting distortion of my needs does not, and cannot, excuse me from any chain of consequences I set in motion by an unwise choice or action.

I am at peace with myself to the degree that I recognize my own feelings and urges and accept my innate authority to handle them — that I consciously take charge of my own needs and motivations. I benefit to the extent that I discharge my personal responsibilities with perception and wisdom.

My *actions* are not *me.* They are but the manifestations of my current Awareness — but the *methods* I choose to fulfill my prevailing *needs.* My needs, themselves, are largely determined by my state of Awareness.

Regardless of my errors, I invariably do the best my prevailing Awareness and needs, distorted though they may be, MOTIVATE me to do. Condemnation, shame and guilt are totally invalid since I can do only what my Awareness and needs *dictate.* For it is *impossible* to do other than what one *most* wants to do, despite moral values and personal obligations.

Even though I may not approve of my thoughts or actions, I reject all self-condemnation and actively purge my consciousness of any shame, blame, guilt or remorse, for I realize that I invariably do the best I can *at the time* and no one can do better than his best. So rather than *condone* or *condemn* my own or another's mistakes, I search out the causes and then endeavor to improve my motivation through a *greater Awareness* of relevant factors.

If my limited Awareness beclouds the issues and distorts my needs, and thus my *motivation,* this is the *reality* with which I must deal, regardless of "ifs," "oughts" and "musts." I can function harmoniously and effectively only to the degree that I anticipate the total consequences of my proposed acts.

If I am "hurting," there is something I am resisting, not seeing clearly or not doing appropriately; and it is my individual responsibility to determine what this is and correct it.

Blaming another is destructive to my sense of worth, for it means that I am not capable of taking full responsibility for my own ideas, attitudes and actions. It deprives me of a sense of inadequacy and satisfying Self-Esteem.

What another thinks or says, or how well or how poorly he does, cannot make me "less" or "more." I rise or fall according to the wisdom or unwisdom of *my own acts*. I can only stand firm on my own two feet. And if I wish to change, I must chart a new course from where I *now am*.

For good or ill the choice is mine. There are always alternatives, and if I am to live harmoniously and effectively, it is up to me, and me alone, to choose wisely. I need recognize both the benefits and the price demanded for each and then consciously determine (1) am I willing to pay the price? and (2) can I afford it?

Neither I nor others have any right to demand that I be *perfect*. I learn primarily by "doing." And in the final analysis I have only myself to answer to, for I am directly responsible only for *my own* life.

I am infinitely more than my mind, body and actions. In essence, I am a non-physical being, ever doing the best my current Awareness allows, ever growing in understanding and love. Neither praise nor blame, neither the excellence or shortcomings of another, can possibly affect *my* innate worth and importance.

If I am to be happy and at peace, I must accept and be kind and loving toward *myself*. I must allow both myself and others the *freedom* to be "wrong" — to make mistakes, to fail, to be considerably less than perfect in our endeavors and conduct.

Only through increasing my Awareness can I function more harmoniously and effectively — can I achieve constructive goals and greater Self-Esteem, and thereby lead a happy, more self-fulfilling life. Only thus can I become a more loving and consequently a more loved individual. Thus, it is not *what I do*, but my *progress* in increased Awareness that is of fundamental importance in my life. This I can best accomplish by refusing all self-condemnation and shame as I honestly and objectively analyze and evaluate my motivations, reactions, values, assumptions, beliefs, moods and attitudes.

The *hope of mankind*, itself, is increased *individual* Awareness — a deep realization that, in essence we are non-physical entities — each a part of the same cosmic whole, no one *inherently* better or worse than another — each doing the best his prevailing Awareness and distorted needs permit — each inevitably making mistakes in his learning and growth. If there is to be peace and love in the world, there must be peace and love *within* the individuals who people it, and this can only be achieved through loving acceptance of one's own true self, regardless of his mistakes and human frailties.

TEN POINTS TO REMEMBER IN BUILDING SOUND SELF-ESTEEM

1. *I am not my actions* — I am *that which acts*. Thus I have no need to "prove myself" by my accomplishments. My actions are simply the *means* my awareness selects to *fulfill my needs*.

2. My decisions and actions are *completely determined* by my *prevailing Awareness*. I can do nothing my Awareness does not motivate me to do.

3. My Awareness is the *degree of clarity* with which I *perceive* and *understand*, both consciously and non-consciously, *everything that affects my life*.

4. My Awareness simply is *what it is* — the *automatic product* of my total life experience and everything I brought into the world with me. At the *instant* of any decision it is absolutely *fixed*.

5. I invariably do the absolute *best* my prevailing Awareness permits, for my Awareness literally *dictates* my every choice and decision. Knowing that I *always do what I "have to do" at the time,* I am free of shame, blame, guilt and remorse.

6. *I am fully responsible* for my life and well-being for *I* benefit or suffer according to the consequences of my every decision and action.

7. *I am the final authority* for everything I say and do, for I alone am responsible for the resulting consequences. I must be in full charge of my life and affairs if I am to have sound Self-Esteem.

8. It behooves me to continually *expand my Awareness,* for my only limitation is my individual level of Awareness — since it is my prevailing Awareness that determines the *wisdom or un-wisdom of everything I do*.

9. Any mistakes I make are but *stepping stones* in my learning and growth — in the *expansion of my Awareness*.

10. No one is *one iota* more or less worthy, more or less important that I am, for everyone is *innately worthy* and *important* in the scheme of things — his ability and wisdom varying only according to his prevailing state of Awareness.

REMEMBER

SELF-ESTEEM: Our Self-Esteem is an emotion — not an intellectual inventory of our favorable characteristics, but how warm, friendly and appreciative we actually feel toward ourselves. It is the degree that we consciously or non-consciously accept and like ourselves, despite our mistakes and human frailties. It is *not* egotism!

AWARENESS: Our Awareness is the clarity with which we perceive and understand, both consciously and non-consciously, everything that affects our lives. It is the automatic product of our total heritage and entire life experience.

MOTIVATION: Our Motivation is a conscious or non-conscious desire sufficiently intense to initiate fulfillment. It is what we most want to do at the time, i.e., what we would rather do than not do. It may or may not cause enjoyment, but it is the only reason possible for doing anything.

ACTIONS: Our actions are simply the *means* our Awareness selects for satisfying our *needs*. They are neither "good" nor "bad" — they are simply wise or unwise, depending on the extent that our particular needs, or the means our Awareness chooses to fulfill those needs, are *distorted*, i.e., out of alignment with reality.

SOMETHING TO PONDER

As evident in the "Realities of Human Behavior," we are not our actions; neither are we our Awareness. Who or what, then, are we? If you do not already have a comfortable answer to the question, Who am I?, perhaps the following article *"WHO AM I?"* may help you resolve the problem. In any event it is of vital importance to your self-esteem that you do have a satisfying answer to this question. Do not, however, accept my answer — or anyone else's — without careful consideration.

I suggest that after thoughtful reading of the following article you sit quietly for a few minutes, still the turmoil of your mind — and quietly question and listen to the inner wisdom ever waiting on the threshold of your consciousness. For the answers lie within — and they will come through, if you give them sufficient opportunity.

WHO AM I?

A sculptor, asked how he sculpted such a beautiful elephant, answered, "I just chipped away all the marble that did not look like an elephant." In a similar way we can, perhaps, find our real selves by eliminating what is not truly us. Let us examine the possibilities:

Am I my actions? No, I am not my actions; I am that which acts. My actions are but the means I choose to fulfill my needs. They are but manifestations of my prevailing awareness, for both my needs and how I choose to fulfill them, are determined by my awareness.

Am I my body? No, I am not my body for I can lose both arms and legs, as well as many other parts, without being diminished as an individual. My body is merely the instrument or means through which I function in this material phase of my existence. Even though my body be wasted away to the point of death, I am still *me* — as much as I ever was.

Am I my mind? No, I am not my mind. For my mind is but a human computer that receives the data of my five senses. My mind is the instrument through which my awareness functions.

Am I my awareness? No, I am not my awareness. I am that which is aware. My awareness is but the automatic product of my heritage and total life experience, including my total conditioning. My awareness acts as my deputy self, my commander-in-chief, for I function through my awareness. If I *were* my awareness I would cease to be every time I fell into a dreamless sleep.

Am I my ego? No, I am not my ego. My ego is but my innate drive to fulfill my basic need — my fundamental need to "feel good," physically, mentally and emotionally. It responds to the tensions generated by my desires, no matter how distorted or destructive such desires may be, owing to my limited and often distorted awareness. The greater my self-esteem, the better I feel toward myself and my environment, the less need for my ego to manifest itself.

Then what am I? I am a unique and precious being — a nonphysical essence. My awareness tells me, "I am" — of this I have no doubt. Therefore I must be a non-physical essence, a part of all Life. My awareness shows me that I am unique, for no one has exactly the same heritage, background and awareness as I. All my experience, especially my problems and mistakes, is continually adding to my awareness. Since life is of ultimate importance, I *am* a unique and precious being, ever learning and growing. And the greater my awareness, the greater is my capacity for love and enjoyment of life. And the more richly I enjoy life, the more eager and able I am to contribute to the well-being of those around me.

I am often asked, "What is *your* answer to the question *Who am I?*" Thus, for whatever it may be worth, I offer my personal convictions. But please bear in mind that what is "right" for me may or may not be "right" for you. Only you yourself can determine the right answer for you.

I believe that there are two aspects to every human being. There is the inner being, the real self or soul, which is an individualized part of Infinite Spirit, or God. There is the surface being or ego self, which is but the surface manifestation of the real self. It is this ego self that must learn and grow, expand its Awareness, so that it can eventually become fully aware of its nature and being. I perceive the ego to be but an expression of the ego self's need and drive to express, and thereby expand the Awareness of the surface being so that it can ultimately achieve complete self-realization.

I believe that in an ultimate sense, *every experience is "good,"* for everything in our trial and error search for reality contributes to our learning and growth. To me the meaning and purpose of life is the expansion of our Awareness, and that besides this expansion and our inner need to love and serve our fellowman, everything else in our lives is relatively unimportant.

Should you accept the essence of this belief, how can you do less than *love yourself as an eternal and precious part of God?*

To "feel good," thus to achieve genuine success and happiness, we must come to terms with our repressed and thwarted needs. Our deep need to know *who we are, why we are here* and *where we are going* is ever pressing from within for recognition and fulfillment. It is this repressed and hidden need that robs us of inner peace and contentment, for everyone's deepest, most pressing, and usually most unrecognized need is his spiritual unfoldment. And you cannot achieve truly sound self-esteem until you accept and meet this challenge to discover who you really are. For only then will you *know beyond question* your true worth and importance!

OBSERVABLE FACTS

1. *SELF-ACCEPTANCE:* Others accept you at your own evaluation; if you devaluate yourself, so also must others. Do not be harsh and demanding with yourself. Allow yourself your mistakes and human frailties. Remember *you are not your actions* and the more warm and loving you are to yourself the better you will feel — the more you will enjoy life and the more warm and loving you will be to others. And this makes life rich and meaningful. You can't be bored or depressed when you truly accept and appreciate yourself.

2. *SELFISHNESS:* You are inherently selfish since your basic need and motivation is to "feel good," and since your number one responsibility is your own growth and well-being. This does not, however, mean that you must be aggressive, greedy and uncaring about the needs and problems of others. There is no such thing as "altruism." The only possible reason for doing anything is that you would rather do it than not do it for your own sense of well-being.

3. *LOVING RELATIONSHIPS:* You can genuinely love and care for others only to the degree that you love and care for yourself. With good Self-Esteem, you will naturally be loving and caring.

4. *RESENTMENT:* You don't have to enjoy being with everyone you meet or know. For you may not have similar interests and values or you may not like another's life style. If, however, you actively dislike, hate or resent anyone, you definitely have a serious problem in Awareness. You are overlooking the fact that everyone is invariably doing what he has to do, and therefore the BEST he can do at the time. All resentment and condemnatory "oughts," "shoulds" and "musts" stem from imposing our own values and expectations on another who must inevitably act and react according to *his* "individual Awareness."

5. *VULNERABILITY:* You are not actually vulnerable to the remarks, opinions and attitudes of others. It is only your low Self-Esteem that does not allow you to accept your own worth, authority and wisdom over theirs. Furthermore, you are not your opinions and actions, the "real you" cannot even be touched, much less hurt or damaged.

6. *FREEDOM TO BE "WRONG":* If you can accept your own mistakes and shortcomings, if you can allow yourself to be "wrong," free of condemnation, shame or guilt, you can then allow others to "be wrong," to "goof up," without blaming them or trying to "straighten them out." It is when you, yourself, feel inadequate and inferior that you endeavor to "make yourself right" by making others "wrong."

7. *COMPARISONS:* Comparisons for the purpose of establishing your relative worth or merit are absolutely meaningless, for no two people have the same background, abilities and Awareness. Furthermore, you are not your talents or actions. You can perform only as well as your Awareness permits — and your individual Awareness simply is what it is!

8. *RESISTANCE AND REBELLION:* Resistance to anything you cannot change is not only futile but also very hurtful. It causes more emotional turmoil and suffering than almost anything you can do — it even intensifies physical pain. This and self-pity are two prime ingredients of grief for the loss of a loved one. If you can change what you are resisting, do so, otherwise, accept and live with it.

45

Rebellion for the sake of rebellion stems from the frustration of resisting your inability to do what *you* want to do, or what you personally consider "ought" or "should" be, regardless of unalterable circumstances.

9. *PROMISES AND COMMITMENTS:* Promises and commitments, even the marriage contract, should be considered at best no more than a sincere statement of intent. For as our Awareness changes so do our needs, and we may no longer have a need for that particular thing or relationship. This is not telling you what "should" be, but how it actually is. If a person's value to honor his commitment is stronger than a conflicting need to do otherwise, well and good. It is wise, however, to realize that for you to "know better" is not sufficient for you to "do better" if you have a conflicting need that outweighs your value to "do better." Witness the alcoholic, chain smoker and compulsive over-eater.

10. *EXPECTATIONS:* Much unhappiness stems from thwarted expectations. Expectations based on how another person should, or is going to act, can cause much disappointment and bitterness. Such expectations can be very illusory, for no one has the same Awareness and thus it is an impossibility to "put yourself in someone else's shoes." When you entertain a certain expectation, realize that it may be based on false assumptions and face the possibility of being disappointed with equanimity — knowing that everyone must do what his individual Awareness dictates, however limited or distorted his Awareness may be.

11. *REWARD AND PUNISHMENT:* Since everyone must inevitably do what his Awareness dictates, i.e., what he *has to do* at the time, and since he cannot be held responsible for his degree of Awareness (it being the automatic product of his heritage and total life conditioning), there is no rational justification for either reward or punishment. The only sure reward is in the "feel good" of your act. *You are asking for disappointment if you do something because you expect something in return.* For the "return" depends on the other person's Awareness, which may be quite different from what you expected. A reward may be given as an incentive to encourage certain action, but this is something else again.

While it may be necessary to incarcerate someone for the safety of society or for rehabilitation purposes, punishment as revenge or as a punitive measure, e.g., to make one "pay his debt to society," is totally unjustified. We might, with comparable logic, jail or execute a child for an act he committed out of ignorance. For a limited or distorted Awareness *is* ignorance of the realities of life and its cause and effect relationships.

12. *DESTROY YOUR SELF-IMAGE:* An image of the "kind of guy I am" can be very restrictive and also keep you from relating openly with others. It keeps you from being "real." Destroy any such image and be your own wonderful self — free to change anything, including your concepts, values and opinions at an instant's notice. You will experience much greater freedom, self-satisfaction — and Self-Esteem.

13. *LIVE IN THE PRESENT INSTANT:* The only living time is NOW. If you use the present merely as a bridge between remorse or regret for the past and anxiety for the future — or simply live till WHEN, "when my ship comes in," etc., you will find life bleak and depressing. Program yourself to be keenly aware and concerned with the "here and now" rather than with the "when" or "then." Self-Esteem can only be experienced in the present instant.

14. *DO NOT ACCEPT REJECTION:* Do not assume that there is something wrong with you simply because someone prefers another, or another's company over yours. We all have different conditioning – different interests, values, likes and dislikes. So don't take it personally, allow everyone the freedom of his own Awareness, to do as he sees fit. And do not accept another's judgments and authority over your own. At the very worst *you* cannot be rejected – only your personality is at stake, which is no more nor less than a reflection of your own individual Awareness.

15. *DO NOT INDULGE IN SELF-PITY:* Self-pity is perhaps the most destructive emotion in which you can indulge. No one ever promised you that life would be a "bed of roses." Be willing to accept life's cards as they are dealt, knowing that every painful experience is for your needed learning and growth and a challenge to your Awareness – and make every effort to get the most out of it. In case of grief, it's fine to go with your emotions and let them run themselves out – every emotion, that is, except self-pity, for self-pity will lock in your grief and misery.

16. *COMPASSION:* If we really understand the "Realities of Human Behavior," compassion is an automatic reaction toward those who are suffering, even though they have brought it on themselves through self-indulgence, dishonesty, greed, murder or whatever. For we each have to do what our individual Awareness compels us to do, however distorted the action or disastrous the consequences. From this it is evident that it is only circumstances and our greater Awareness (for which we, ourselves, can take no credit), that has kept each of us out of similar situations.

17. *HUMILITY:* Humility, the lack of self-exaltation, is a natural state of being when we have sufficient Awareness to realize that we, ourselves, can take no credit for the enviable or exemplary aspects of our lives – that it is only the good fortune of our greater Awareness that is responsible for such desirable conditions. This does not, however, imply that an egotist should be censured, for he too, is doing what his limited Awareness dictates.

18. *SELF-RIGHTEOUSNESS:* Self-righteousness is not only totally unfounded, since we each do what we have to do, but there is probably nothing that will make us more unacceptable and more avoided in social gatherings. This, again, is a symptom of identifying ourselves with our actions. Self-righteousness demonstrates that our Awareness is sadly distorted relative to the realities of human behavior.

19. *IT'S ALL IN HOW YOU HANDLE IT:* From the foregoing, it is easy to see that it is not what happens to you but how you handle it – your emotional reactions and attitudes that determine your degree of misery or joy.

20. *LIFE CAN BE A BALL:* Our natural state of being is inner peace and joy, and all-encompassing love. If we are not appreciative and loving of ourselves, our fellowmen and the tremendous world around us, it can only be because of our limited and distorted Awareness. In this case our perspective is faulty and we are out of alignment with "what is." The simple truth is, if you are "hurting" you are doing something "wrong." Although we are all subject to "growing pains," if we do not intelligently deal with them, we will continue to suffer. We can greatly minimize their frequency and duration through a value-free probing examination of the "pain." We can thus discover the source and cause and thereby deal with it intelligently and effectively.

21. *LOVING YOURSELF:* The more you love yourself the more you will love others and the world about you. And the more you love, the more others will love you -- and the richer and more meaningful your life will be - the more you will appreciate the beauty and the wonder all about you! The fundamental ingredient of love is the total unconditional acceptance of the object of your love. True, undistorted love is the most wonderful and precious thing in life. If it is possessive, demanding or controlling it is *not* true love. For undistorted love is as fresh and free as a mountain breeze.

22. *FOR HAPPINESS AND CONTENTMENT:*

(1) We need a sense of "belonging" and an appreciation of our innate worth and importance in the scheme of things.

(2) We need to relate with others. We need to love and be loved.

(3) We need a sense of meaning and purpose in our lives.

(4) We need to realize that *we are not our actions* -- that despite our mistakes, defeats and failures we invariably *do the best we can possibly do* at the time.

23. *THE CHOICE IS YOURS:* Aside from low Self-Esteem, most of our hurting stems from resisting "what is," instead of accepting what we cannot change. The choice is ours; we can either make friends with life or be "destroyed" by it. We can choose the "easy way" of personal growth, i.e., being accepting, relaxed and receptive, and thus tune in to our infallible inner wisdom, or we can resist and willfully demand our own way with life and suffer the resulting cause and effect "lumps on our head," which literally force us into greater Awareness and ultimate alignment with reality. For life is a school - a school for increasing our Awareness of Reality. The choice is ever ours, the *problem* is to gain sufficient Awareness to consistently make a *wise choice.*

WE ARE NOT OUR ACTIONS: We are that which acts. Our actions are but the means determined by our Awareness for fulfilling our needs. We can think, speak and act *only as wisely as our prevailing Awareness permits.*

We each invariably do what our Awareness dictates, i.e., what we have to do at the time.

Remember, our Awareness is the *automatic* product of our heritage and total conditioning, and at the instant of any act or decision it is absolutely fixed. It simply *is what it is* at the time.

EIGHTEEN WAYS OF
PERPETUATING LOW SELF-ESTEEM

1. Identifying with your actions rather than your non-physical essence — lack of realization that you are a unique and precious being, however unwise or inadequate your actions.

2. Not being in conscious charge of your own life and not accepting full responsibility for your own growth and total well-being, regardless of handicapping circumstances beyond your control.

3. Not having and actively pursuing a life objective that is meaningful to you, lack of clear-cut and meaningful goals to guide your decisions and preclude "coasting," self-indulgence, procrastination and lack of self-discipline.

4. Not recognizing and exercising your inherent authority over your own life and affairs — not doing your own thinking and making your own decisions — requiring the permission, confirmation, and agreement of others for what you think, say and do.

5. Being a "professional people pleaser."

6. Working at an occupation that you heartily dislike, especially one that is not meaningful to you.

7. Neglecting or ignoring your own needs in order to "serve" others — not recognizing and accepting your own growth and well-being as your number one responsibility.

8. Not realizing that you are invariably doing the best you can possibly do at the time, regardless of your mistakes, unacceptable behavior or human frailties.

9. Harboring shame, guilt and remorse — and/or self-pity.

10. Indulging in destructive criticism and self-accusation — belittling and condemning yourself for your mistakes and failures.

11. Depending on others for a sense of importance and realness rather than realizing that everyone is of equal worth and importance not recognizing that we vary only in our individual awareness — in our specific talents and capabilities.

12. Not allowing yourself the right and freedom of full expression — not "doing your own thing" — not developing your innate talents and capabilities.

13. Not following your endeavors through to a logical conclusion, i.e., "giving up," before the job is finished.

14. Comparing yourself and your accomplishments, i.e., your actions, with those of others as a gauge of your individual worth and importance. Having a conviction that you must prove your worth through superior performance and achievements.

15. Not speaking up for your own convictions, letting others ignore and belittle you. Not realizing that no one can insult or "put you down" unless you accept his worth and authority over your own.

16. Depending on others for doing things that you are capable of doing for yourself.

17. Not realizing that your very existence proves your innate worth and importance, regardless of how well or how poorly you conform to accepted standards.

18. In short, not thoroughly understanding and being aware of the "Realities of Human Behavior" *and acting accordingly — especially* continuing to VALUE JUDGE *yourself* for every mistake, shortcoming, defeat and human frailty.

Since you cannot escape the consequences, and therefore the responsibility for your actions, you are the final authority for your every thought, word and deed. Therefore exercise this authority and consciously take full charge of your own life and affairs. It is much better for your Self-Esteem to make mistakes through unwise decisions than to fail by default.

Why should we *praise* or *condemn — reward* or *punish* one for saying or doing what his current awareness *compels* him to? Especially when we know that one's awareness is the *automatic* product of his *heritage* and *total conditioning —* that at any given instant it simply *is what it is,* and therefore subject to neither credit nor blame.

Praise without blame is like a stick with only one end, for we cannot justify either without, at the same time, validating the other. Neither has any more reality than a coin with only one side. Recognition and appreciation, however, are both valid and constructive actions, and therefore highly desirable.

The act of drinking a cup of coffee is mute evidence that a man is not his actions — that he is merely satisfying his need or desire for a drink of coffee. Is he any more his actions, if in anger, he throws it in another's face? Is this action not also simply a means of satisfying his dominant need, even though it is distorted?

In appraising one's character, it is not the action but the motivation that counts.

Humility and gratitude are *natural* reactions for an aware person toward his outstanding characteristics and achievements. For he realizes that it is only his Awareness that is responsible — and that for his *Awareness* he can claim no credit.

You can only succeed in building sound self-esteem by having sufficient motivation, maintaining a clear vision of its achievement, and persevering with faith in its accomplishment.

PARENT'S PRAYER
(Adapted)

Our ever loving Father, help me to be a better parent.

Teach me to understand my children, to listen patiently to what they say, and to answer their questions wisely.

May I be ever conscious that they are not their actions — that any faults or mistakes lie not with them, but with their limited awareness.

Help me keep from interrupting or contradicting them — to be as kind and courteous to them as I would have them be to me — to treat them as I would a treasured friend.

Forbid that I should ever laugh at their mistakes, or resort to shame or ridicule should they displease me.

May I never punish them for my selfish satisfaction or to show my superior power, and may I never tempt them to lie, cheat or steal.

Guide me hour-by-hour, that I may demonstrate by all I say and do that love, honesty, self-discipline and appreciation of self produce happiness.

When out of sorts, help me, O Lord, to hold my tongue — to be consistent, wise and just; kind and loving in all situations.

May I be ever mindful that my children are children and not expect them to act and react as adults.

Let me not rob them of the opportunity to do what they can for themselves, to make their own decisions and suffer their own mistakes.

May I never judge their worth by their actions or by comparisons with others.

Give me the awareness to grant their reasonable requests and the courage to deny requests that would do them harm.

Help me to teach them sound values, responsibility and self-discipline, yet keep them free from self-accusation, shame, guilt and remorse.

May I teach them to be self-reliant and immune to the negative opinions and attitudes of others.

May I discipline them through an increased awareness, love and unwavering firmness rather than through reward and punishment.

Bless them with the awareness to recognize and accept the reality of all situations — to appreciate their own unique being, their innate worth and importance in the scheme of things.

Help me, O Lord, to allow them to be *themselves* — to show my appreciation and to inculcate them with sound Self-Esteem and the *joy of living!*

SUGGESTIONS FOR SUCCESSFUL PARENTING

1. Be kind and loving to yourself so that you can be kind and loving to your child. The parents' sound Self-Esteem is an essential requirement for inculcating sound Self-Esteem in their children. A parent with low self-esteem and resulting life style is a destructive model for the child.

2. Remember your child does not have the same Awareness as you.

3. Be ever aware that your child is not his actions — that he is not "bad" because he behaves other than you or others think he should.

4. Do not motivate your child by reward and punishment. Motivate him to the desired action, if such action is sound, through exposing his Awareness to the pros and cons of the particular action, rather than through fear of punishment. If, however, you cannot motivate him by such means, withhold valued privileges, but only as a training measure — never as a punishment for his act. And see that your child understands the difference.

5. Show your child the same respect, consideration and kindness that you would show a valued friend. Treat him as *you* would like to be treated.

6. Teach him sound values, the "Realities of Human Behavior" and how to act in order to build and maintain sound Self-Esteem.

7. See that he takes as much responsibility for his own life and well-being as his current age and Awareness permit.

8. Never do anything, including making decisions, for your child that he is capable of doing for himself — other than perhaps an occasional favor.

9. Show him by your attitude, speech and *action* that he is a unique and precious being. Discipline (i.e., motivate) him with specific reasons — with love and understanding.

10. Give him every opportunity to learn and grow. Allow him the opportunity and freedom to make mistakes but see that he profits from such mistakes, free of condemnation, shame, blame and guilt.

11. Do not be possessive. Hold your child to you as gently and *lightly* as you would a butterfly; he does not *belong* to you, rather he came *through* you.

12. Be as open and honest with him as you would be with a trusted confidant.

13. Deal with him as an equal. Adults are but children with more extensive conditioning — not necessarily all "good!"

14. Let him know that you are human and therefore fallible — that you too make mistakes and survive — that mistakes are part of a normal learning curve.

15. Do not demand his love and affection — endeavor to earn it. He *owes you nothing* — he did not ask you to bring him into the world. The only justifiable reward for raising a child lies in the "feel good" of doing an exemplary job. The better job you do, the better your child will feel and act toward you as he reaches "maturity."

16. Teach your child the fallacy of self-accusation and condemnation — see that he does not condemn himself for his mistakes — that he does not harbor shame, guilt or remorse.

17. Do not equivocate; tell your child "yes" or "no" with reasoned conviction — alter your mind only if a change in your Awareness so dictates.

18. Do not be too permissive or too controlling! If you do, the relationship is almost sure to backfire during adolescence. In any case, you will seriously damage your child's self-esteem.

19. Teach him that both sex and death are "good" and natural parts of life, and thus freely open to questioning and discussion.

20. If your personal belief permits, teach him that he is a nonphysical essence, inviolable, invincible and eternal.

21. Be aware of your opportunity and responsibility to lead your child from a state of total dependency to one of complete independence, so that he may become a responsible, free and happy individual.

22. Listen to your child's questions and ideas with sincere interest and respond to him as you would to one of your own age, but in terms he can understand.

23. Be aware of and respect his needs. In case you do not feel free to satisfy a particular need or desire, explain your reasons in terms he can understand and accept.

24. Teach him to understand and respect *your* needs. Do not allow him to tyrannize you.

25. Do not be harsh and demanding with your child. Do not insist on unrealistic standards of performance, or raise new standards before he has learned to handle the present ones. Remember that he is not his actions and that he is doing the best his current awareness permits. If his behavior is unsatisfactory do not scold — work on expanding his awareness in the indicated areas. Assure him that you love and cherish him regardless of any unwise acts.

26. Encourage him to express his negative and "unacceptable" emotions (as well as his positive and "acceptable" emotions) without fear of censure but as appropriately as possible.

27. Impress him at every opportunity that he is not his actions. Reward and punishment, for example, cause him to identify with his actions and feel "less than" when he makes a mistake.

28. Teach him the irrationality and destructiveness of competition as a means of gaining self-worth. (One can do only what his individual awareness enables him to do — there is no rational justification for *either* credit or blame.)

29. Do not compare your child's unsatisfactory behavior or lack of achievement with that of his peers, particularly that of a more gifted brother or sister. Let him know you love and value him for his intrinsic worth as a unique and precious being — not for how well he behaves or what he can achieve.

30. Do not expect too much of your child — do not force him beyond his capacity to deliver. Teach him that defeats and shortcomings do not make him "less than" or a failure — that everyone is inherently equal regardless of race, creed, color, possessions, power or "prestige."

31. Teach your child the relative unimportance of physical characteristics. True beauty arises from within and expresses itself through the eyes and countenance, through one's voice and behavior.

32. Above all, keep in mind that sound self-esteem is the most precious gift you can possibly give your child — and *act accordingly!*

COMPANIONSHIP

When with a brother,
    And we are all brothers,

Talk not always of things serious and requisite
    But respond to the spirit of him with whom you speak,

And be he light and carefree, be you likewise.
    But be receptive to his inner nature

And partake of his wisdom and love.
    Should you sense a yearning

Give him a glimpse of the flower of *your* dreams.
    But if he responds not to its beauty and fragrance

Go blissfully on your way. However,
    Should he be struck with the allure of the blossom

Show him freely all the wonderful flowers of your garden.
    And speak with him of the invisible Divinity which

Encompasses and interpenetrates us all,
    And let him feel the love you bear him

As a brother and a precious child of God,
    On his lonesome journey to self-knowledge and freedom.

Lilburn S. Barksdale

SUGGESTIONS FOR A HAPPY MARRIAGE

Aside from mutual love and respect, the most crucial requirement for an enduring and happy marriage is the sound Self-Esteem of both husband and wife. In fact, without adequate Self-Esteem, it will be impossible for the marriage partners to implement many of the following suggestions:

1. Thoroughly understand and internalize the "Realities of Human Behavior."

2. A successful marriage must be nourished and cared for. Continue to show each other the same love and consideration you did during courtship.

3. Certainly the basic rule for a good marriage relationship is the "Golden Rule" — i.e., treat the other in all ways as *you* would like to be treated.

4. Make the "Life Style" program a consistent way of life.

5. Do not impose your value system on your mate.

6. Give your spouse the same courtesy and freedom you like to be given.

7. Do not try to make yourself "right" by making your mate "wrong."

8. Do not try to dominate or possess. Maintain a sense of your individual worth and importance and you will have no need for such behavior. Everyone has a vital need to express according to his own nature and inner urging.

9. Treat each other as equals on an equal basis.

10. Share your joys and sorrows, your work and play — your victories and defeats.

11. Do not surrender responsibility and authority for your individual growth and well-being, or usurp your partner's responsibility and authority for his growth and well-being.

12. Be frank and open, honest and sincere with each other at all times. Drop all masks and barriers.

13. Look after your own needs as well as those of your mate.

14. Be authentic — be yourself at all costs and encourage your partner to do likewise. Scrap any self-image that interferes with your being "you."

15. Your marriage can be no better than your sense of inner freedom and emotional well-being. To the degree that you (or your spouse) are emotionally sick, will your marriage relationship cause emotional turmoil and suffering.

16. Take a genuine interest in each other's work, hobbies, and extracurricular activities.

17. Do not expect external rewards for your thoughtful and generous acts. Either the reward is in the "feel good" of the act or it is better left undone.

18. Whatever you do, do not indulge in self-pity for the way you are treated by your spouse. Remember you possess the ultimate authority and responsibility for your own well-being; the choice is always yours, even though you may wish to maintain the status quo rather than pay the price demanded for a desired change.

19. Do not allow marital problems to accumulate — handle them one at a time as they occur. Do not build up a head of steam that will explode at an inopportune time. Keep the lid of the tea kettle cracked so that hostility and resentment can dissipate as it is generated. Remember that "fair" and "unfair," "right" and "wrong," are but descriptive terms. Everyone has to do what his Awareness dictates at the time, whether you like it or not. If things become too unpleasant or intolerable, look to your partner's Awareness, not his actions, for a solution.

20. Never be a "nagger" or "complainer." You cannot successfully motivate anyone through "nagging." To be constructively motivated, an individual must be made aware of the potential benefits. If one truly loves the other, the benefit is usually the "feel good" of doing something "nice" for the other. Such feelings, however, need to be nourished by the appreciation of the recipient. Actually, nagging and fault finding are liable to motivate the other to repudiate the "contract" rather than grow closer or uphold the relationship. Love and respect need to be nurtured, not harassed. Thus, resolve all resistance and resentment as they occur.

21. Remember that no marriage contract can be anything more than a sincere statement of intent. It is not a certificate of ownership and it is "good" only as long as an honest and caring relationship exists.

22. Do not expect anything from your spouse that his or her Awareness cannot deliver.

23. Do not indulge in destructive criticism and accusations. Remember that regardless of the act, your partner did what he or she had to at the time.

24. Do not harbor shame, guilt, or remorse, and do nothing to inflict them on your mate.

25. Do not compete with your spouse. Remember you cannot make yourself "more than" or "less than" by your actions, no matter how superior you act or what you achieve. You can only demonstrate your current state of awareness, which is no credit to you, however true to reality it may be.

26. Do not harbor resistance. If it is desirable to change something, proceed if possible to change it. If it is something beyond your power to change, accept it, knowing that situations are "what they are" and that everyone does what he has to do at the time. Is not your mate's love more precious and important than the thing you resist or resent?

27. Do not harbor resentment because your mate does not do what he "should," "ought," or "must." Resentment stems from imposing your particular values on another. Remember, no two people have the same awareness and thus, no one else has the same system of values as you. If you think your mate is "wrong" or "unfair," in spite of being exposed to your views and values, try an alternate solution. But, do not "stew" in resentment, for your mate has to do what his current awareness dictates, regardless of your ideas of "right" and "wrong." Chronic resentment will only destroy your marriage.

28. A marriage requires thought and effort and a good measure of "give and take" if it is to be successful. Do not, however, deny your needs at the expense of your innate dignity or self-respect. There is, however, hardly anything that you cannot do for your mate without injury to your self-esteem if you will do it in the spirit of making a "gift" — an act of your own choice, instead of feeling "trapped" or forced into the action. Avoid resistance by making a "gift" of anything you might otherwise consider a duty or obligation.

29. Maintain a "clear picture" and consciousness of a happy, harmonious marriage and if you can, regularly affirm such a relationship. In any event, if the marriage is important, provide the effort and imagination required to make it work. If it is not worth the time and effort to nurture it, the marriage has small chance of succeeding. The choice is yours.

30. Do not use sex as a control or trading device — or merely for the quick satisfaction of a physical need. Use it for the most tender, intimate expression of your love and caring — the ultimate in togetherness. Above all treat sex as a natural and healthy function, free of any prudery or self-consciousness.

31. Do not allow your mate to take you for granted.

By far the greatest number of divorces and broken homes stem from an inadequate or crippling Self-Esteem. Look at its destruction all about you; and strive unceasingly for sound Self-Esteem if you want to insure a rich and happy marriage.

It is not what happens to us but our resulting reactions and attitudes that determine our joy or sorrow.

If you are not happy, you are doing something "wrong" — something out of alignment with reality.

Everyone is doing the very best his prevailing awareness permits. How then can we judge or condemn him?

Instead of feeling guilty or "less than" for a mistake, why not simply determine how you could have done "better" and let it go?

Resenting another's words or actions is as foolish as resenting the sun for rising before you wished it to — neither could be helped.

AWARENESS

Man is blessed with an innate appreciation for
The ineffable peace and joy of the simple flow of life
And the magnificence and wonder of its manifestations:
A bright crisp dawn pregnant with countless miracles of a new day;
Dew-drenched grasses and the mystery of awakening flowers;
A barely risen sun, blue sky, and the magic of drifting clouds;
The soft beauty and challenging purity of new-fallen snow
Tracked here and there by a scuttling rabbit or furtive coyote;
Pungent smell of burning wood and cheery crackle of a lusty fire;
Hearty food, clear cold water, and well-earned rest;
The startling glory of a flaming sunset and
The clear air and bright stars of a balmy night;

The cloudless stillness of a summer day and
Aromatic fragrance of pine needles under a hot sun;
Verdant meadow ringed with towering conifers and quivering aspen,
The haunting sweetness of chokecherry blossoms and wild roses,
Clear rocky bed and tree-covered banks of a restless stream;
Darting trout, the brusque chittering of squirrels,
Busy talk of insects and the clear melodious song of birds;
A beckoning rainbow and the freshness of a shower-washed earth;
Wildly galloping calves, a newborn colt on its wobbly legs
And the unbelievable softness of baby chicks;
The ripe silkiness of milkweed seed couched in their bursting pod,
Sweet clover and sharp tang of creosote along a railroad track;

The tenderness and joy bestowed by a child's trusting smile;
Youth's strong fresh beauty, the simple dignity and wisdom of age;
Radiant health and the zest and joy of living;
Mutually treasured friendships; the beauty and ecstasy of love
And the wordless communion of soul-to-soul encounter;
The learning and growth of constant effort —
The satisfaction of refusing to step out of life's procession
Regardless of the wounds and anguish
Suffered in personal unfoldment and quest for self-knowledge;
Discovery of one's inner knowing and freedom,
Faith in the beneficent purpose of life,
And a quiet awareness of God.

Lilburn S. Barksdale

WILL, FREE WILL AND RESPONSIBILITY

During the past one hundred years or more, many large and highly touted volumes have been written by many learned men on the nature and use of will. Notwithstanding, "will" and "will power" are about as sadly and often tragically misunderstood today as they have ever been. Actually, "will" is adequately defined in the following sentence:

> "Will is a *conscious decision* generated by a strong, clear-cut desire and vitalized and reinforced by Awareness of the anticipated benefit(s)."

This is *all* "will" is! When we "will" to do something, we simply *decide* to do whatever it is because we have become totally convinced that we *want* to do it — that the potential benefit is well worth the effort or cost of doing it — in other words, *because we would rather do it than not do it.* We may have come to our decision because we felt impelled to honor a moral value, or on the other hand, our decision may have been to fulfill a conflicting need that outweighed our need to honor a particular moral value. In any event, we "willed" to do something that we would rather do than not do, regardless of the initiating reason. What other reason could there possibly be for doing *anything?*

Naturally, the stronger, more insistent our particular desire, the stronger our "will" to satisfy that desire. It takes only a minimum of looking to perceive that the only basic or ultimate reason for doing *anything* — anything at all — is because we would rather do it than not do it, regardless of the specific reasons. Thus, the term "desire power" is a much more appropriate term than "will power," for again, it is our desire that motivates our *every* action.

By the same token, a "sheer act of will" is only accomplished when an individual is literally *"possessed"* by a clear-cut, over-riding desire and either ignores the cost of its fulfillment or is totally willing to pay it. Thus, a "strong willed" person is simply one with intense desires, i.e., motivation, and a "weak willed" person is merely one without strong desires or motivation to do what society or some authority figure feels he "should" do. The moral connotation comes in when the action in question is considered "morally wrong." Thus, a compulsive smoker is considered to be "weak willed" even though his desire or "will," fostered by his compulsive *need* to smoke, is so intense that he finds himself *unable to quit smoking.* Thus, his "will power" to smoke is more powerful than his "will power" to stop smoking. Since, however, his strong will to smoke does not meet with society's or perhaps his own approval, it is not recognized as "will power." If, on the other hand, his need to stop smoking had overpowered his need to smoke, he would have been praised for his "strong will."

This is, of course, irrational since it is the individual's desire, generated by his prevailing Awareness, that causes him to "will" to smoke or not to smoke — one action is not more praiseworthy as an act of will than the other. It is quite evident from the foregoing that a "sheer act of will" is the result of nothing more nor less than an *intense overriding desire* — and it may be negative and destructive as well as positive and constructive.

Now there are many reasons why we might rather do a certain thing in preference to doing something else at that particular time. Such reasons may stem from one or more causes, but *all* are rooted in our prevailing Awareness. For example, there are five or more reasons (as well as combinations of reasons) why we might want to help a certain individual or to aid our fellowman, i.e.:

(1) To make a good impression and/or get credit from others.

(2) To "store pennies in heaven" for a future reward.

(3) To try for an increment of self-approval and acceptance.

(4) To honor a personal value.

(5) To satisfy an inner urge or need to share because of overflowing love and gratitude.

Regardless of the specific cause or motivation, the crucially important thing to realize *and bear in mind* is that we can do *ONLY* what we *would rather do than not do,* and that it is utterly impossible to do *anything* simply because we or others feel we "should," "must" or "ought to." Thus, it is evident that the secret of all "right" action (i.e., action in alignment with life) lies in our Awareness. For our Awareness *is* the one and *ONLY* source of *ALL* our decisions and actions, good, bad or indifferent, right or wrong, "praiseworthy," "sinful" or "evil" as the case may be. Consequently, our *fundamental* personal responsibility is to expand our individual Awareness so that both we, and our fellowman, can reap the rewards of such enlightened Awareness.

In order to deliberately expand our Awareness, it is only necessary to keenly observe and question our own and others' needs and actions, attitudes, concepts, values, beliefs, assumptions, hopes and aspirations — to read, listen and think — to analyze, correlate and evaluate — to meditate on the good, the true and the beautiful and on the source and meaning of all life.

Now, let's take a look at "free will."

Most thinking people believe in either "free will" or "determinism." These are two vitally important concepts, for to a large degree they are responsible for our basic attitude toward life, and thus they critically affect our individual concept of the purpose and meaning of life. Let us explore these two concepts in relation to our "Realities of Human Behavior." We will start by asking a few rhetorical questions.

Does not free will mean you are free to *do anything you choose?* Yes, for what else could it possibly mean?

Now, what determines what you choose? It is your prevailing Awareness that furnishes the data on which you base your decisions — regardless of what the consequences prove to be!

Now, can you determine or control your Awareness at any given instant? Of course not — your Awareness simply is what it IS at any given time, it being the automatic product of your heritage and total life experience.

But are you not *responsible* for your *Awareness?* Yes, for even though you are subject to neither credit nor blame for the "input," you cannot avoid benefiting or suffering from the "output" of your Awareness, however clear or distorted it may be. In other words, you cannot avoid responsibility for the consequences of your decisions.

Can you determine the *future* "input" and "output" of your Awareness? Yes, to the *degree* that you are *motivated* by your existing level of Awareness — to the degree you are motivated to take *conscious* charge of your own life.

Now, why do we say "conscious charge?" Because, whether you realize it or not — whether you like it or not — you cannot *avoid* being in charge of your own life — even though you may be in charge *by default.* For you cannot possibly escape the impact of your total environment and the manner in which you react to the conditions and situations of your environment — you cannot possibly escape any consequences you set in motion by your actions or reactions!

Now, the question: "Do we in fact *have* 'free will'?" Yes. By definition, the answer is a firm YES! You can readily confirm this fact by checking your own life and affairs. You will find that within your intellectual and physical capabilities you definitely *can do anything you WANT.* But, even though you are free to do *anything* you *want,* you cannot make a decision in a vacuum. What you WANT, except in cases of compulsive or impulsive actions, is determined by weighing the costs and benefits of the different alternatives. Now, we may modify or forego a desired choice because of conditioned inhibitions, the laws of the land, or simply by, "What would they think?" — "they" being your authority figures, family, friends or simply other members of your peer group. The fact remains, YOU CAN DO ANYTHING YOU WANT — *anything at all,* but what you "want" is inevitably determined by the data presented by your prevailing Awareness.

Now, at any given instant, your Awareness is not only *what it is,* but it is also "fixed" or frozen, so that at that particular instant there is one, and only *ONE* thing you can possibly do. Thus it is, per se, the BEST you can possibly do under the prevailing circumstances!

Some of you may say, "Yes, but — they might put me in prison for an illegal act — even execute me." So what! You can still do the thing in question, providing you are *willing to pay the price* — i.e., the penalty demanded for such an antisocial and illegal act. The fact is, "illegal" doesn't mean you *cannot act "illegally"* — it merely means that society exacts a certain price, a penalty for such acts. Thus, there doesn't appear to be any question but that we *do have* "free will" — it's what we do with it that determines our joys and sorrows. Right?

Now, what are the main sources of "input" for expanding your Awareness so that what you choose to do will be more harmonious and acceptable?

(1) Your total environment.

(2) Your inner "knowing," intuition, insight or conscience.

(3) The cause and effect relationships of your every decision and action — plus your observation of the cause and effect relationships all around you.

(4) Self-discovery — recognizing and understanding your needs and motivations — concepts, values, assumptions, ideals and beliefs — your hopes and aspirations — your defenses, aggressions and compulsions — your likes and dislikes — your sense of meaning and purpose of life and the means you choose to fulfill your every need and desire.

Does it not now seem pretty smart to deliberately take active charge of *your own life*, since *you* cannot possibly escape the impact of your environment or the consequences of your actions and reactions? It does appear pretty sensible to "call your own shots" — does it not? Moreover, such responsible action builds Self-Esteem, whereas not being in conscious charge of your own life and affairs seriously injures or actually destroys Self-Esteem.

Now, suppose you *have* decided to take conscious charge of your own life; here are two items of utmost importance to you and to your Self-Esteem.

One is Self-Discipline, and the other — your Life Objectives. Let's first turn our attention to Self-Discipline.

Self-Discipline rests on recognition and exercise of your *innate authority* to accept responsibility for your own life and affairs — on being in *conscious* charge of your life and accepting the consequences of all your decisions and actions, however disastrous they may be. Self-Discipline is primarily a matter of motivation. It is the ability to plan your life and to implement those plans because you are convinced that the benefits of your chosen actions amply outweigh the costs involved. Also, it depends on your ability to say a firm "NO" and mean it, when a "yes" answer would not eventuate in your own best interest. It is the opposite of self-indulgence and drifting — of taking the path of least resistance. Now, we often go contrary to our resolutions and self-interest because the motivation generated by our desire for *future* benefits becomes obscured or overpowered by the pressures exerted by current intense, *conflicting* needs; for example, the appeal of luscious, fattening foods when you are on a strict diet which has been motivated by your long term desire to both *look* and *feel* better in the future. Or, again, you may suddenly decide that the anticipated benefits of a certain objective are not worth the cost of achieving it — of having, for instance, to deny fulfillment of strong conflicting needs — especially if your original objective was based on conditioned "oughts," "shoulds" and "musts" instead of on a clear-cut decision stemming from your own personal conviction. This, incidentally, is why most New Year's resolutions, for instance, to stop drinking, smoking or overeating, "fall by the board."

Self-Discipline, in order to succeed, must be founded on "total decisions," i.e., decisions based on clearly recognized needs that have been carefully investigated as to the benefits and costs involved. Your decision to act in a given manner will then be based on your own conclusion that the potential benefits definitely outweigh all the costs involved and *not* simply decided by your own or society's concept of what you "should" or "should not" do.

To have power, your choice must be based on what you consider to be the best or only way of achieving the desired benefits — plus the fact that you are both completely *willing and able* to pay the price demanded. In other words, lack of Self-Discipline and procrastination are both the result of inadequate or confused motivation. For the sake of your Self-Esteem, it is well to keep in mind that no one can do *anything* without sufficient motivation; and furthermore, that such motivation can be generated only by input to your *Awareness* — there is simply *no other possible source* of personal motivation. For regardless of concepts, moral values or whatever, you can do *only* what *you most want to do* — i.e., *what you would rather do than not do!*

In light of the foregoing, it is easy to see that to *"know better"* is not necessarily sufficient to *"do better."* It is only sufficient when there are no conflicting needs strong enough to overpower your motivation to "do better." Thus, should you find yourself incapable of doing something you feel you *should* do, recognize the cause, let go of your decision to so act and pay whatever price is demanded for not carrying it out. For in so doing, you will drop any resistance and *you will then not fail to act by default.* Instead, you will have simply faced the reality of *what is,* (not what "should" or "ought" to be) and dealt with it in a clear-cut, positive manner. Such action builds Self-Esteem whereas stubbornly holding on and being "niggled" by your "oughts," "shoulds" and "musts" tears it down. So much for Self-Discipline.

Now, let's take a look at Life Objectives. The first requirement is to clarify and *establish* clear-cut life goals. For you cannot achieve either a long range "feel good" or sound Self-Esteem without a meaningful objective in your life. For such an objective is necessary to keep you motivated, as well as to provide you with a sense of progress and a beckoning vision of a meaningful contribution to life. Such a vision is vital to your emotional well-being and zest for life.

Now, to clarify your Life Objective: It is of vital importance if you are to realize such Objective that:

(1) It be of your own choice (not selected to meet someone else's desires or expectations.)

(2) That because of your realistic evaluation of the benefits vs. the costs, you make a conscious, "total" decision to succeed in achieving your objective.

(3) That you maintain a clear vision of achieving such Objective.

A firm commitment to yourself is essential to achieving your Objective. Every night for a full week and at regular periods thereafter, review your day's activities and behavior. Ask yourself:

(1) What, if anything, have I done this day that was out of alignment (in conflict) with my chosen Objective?

(2) What have I done this day (in which I have just invested another day of my life) that has actually contributed to my chosen Objective?

Now, if you really want to feel good about yourself, i.e., raise your Self-Esteem, *every day* make a *meaningful contribution,* however small, to the realization of your chosen Objective.

You will immediately notice a fantastic improvement in both your Self-Esteem and your enjoyment of life, when you establish a truly meaningful Life Objective and conscientiously *work toward its accomplishment.* And again, if you want to "feel good," *every day,* each day of your life, take some new positive action that contributes to this chosen Objective.

If you do not yet have a clearly defined meaningful Life Objective, here is one for your consideration:

Deliberately *expand your Awareness* of both yourself, your inner being and of your total environment, until you habitually experience a harmonious, meaningful and happy life. If you do, you will never be bored and your life will be exhilarating, *constructive* and joyful. What better objective could you have, to what better "feel good" could you aspire? You need never worry about being selfish, for you will automatically share your Awareness and good fortune with an overflowing, grateful heart!

If you are not experiencing life as a "ball," you are doing something "wrong," something out of alignment with reality, with *what IS*. And if you are, the reason is primarily because of your faulty conditioning, of erroneous concepts, values, assumptions and beliefs. Your inharmonious actions and reactions and your resulting negative moods and attitudes arise largely from faulty perception and understanding of the many factors that affect your life.

The most destructive effect of faulty conditioning is low and damaging, often destructive, Self-Esteem. What is meant by Self-Esteem? "Self-Esteem" is how you actually *feel* about yourself, your sense of personal worth — how you value yourself. It is a *feeling*, an emotion based on acceptance of self as an important and worthy individual, despite your mistakes, shortcomings and human frailties. In short, Self-Esteem is *genuine* love of self. It is *not* an intellectual concept of your personal worth or an intellectual evaluation of your pluses and minuses, of your strengths and weaknesses, of your skills or lack of skills. It is not an arbitrary self-image. Above all, it is *not egotism*, for conceit and boasting are but classic *symptoms* of low Self-Esteem. We would have no need to boast and talk about our exploits if we had true self-acceptance, if we truly valued and loved ourselves.

Now, what is the primary source of low Self-Esteem? By far, the most common cause is low Self-Esteem parents, one or both, but especially the mother, for it is with the mother that the child spends his early formative years. The child's intuitive recognition of his parents' sense of insecurity and unworthiness causes the child to feel insecure and unworthy. Lack of self-worth is thus locked in and intensified by the destructive life style engendered by low Self-Esteem parents — the model for the child.

Lack of Self-Esteem is truly the most crucial factor in everyone's life, for practically all our personal problems stem, either directly or indirectly, from a low or crippling Self-Esteem. For example: *Alcoholism* and *drug addiction* are usually the result of an effort to escape a self the individual hates or dislikes, to avoid the misery and emotional hurting engendered by self-rejection. *Alienation* and *isolation* are basically caused by one's withdrawal, caused by a sense of inadequacy. *Anger* is often the result of low Self-Esteem, for it causes us to be unduly upset at ourselves for our all-too-human mistakes, lacks and shortcomings. *Intolerance* of others' differences in values and opinions is caused by a compulsive need for confirmation and agreement, owing to a lack of confidence in ourselves and our values and opinions. *Anxiety* and *worry* are caused by a sense of dependency and lack of confidence in our authority and ability to adequately handle our own lives. *Blaming* and *complaining* result from a refusal to accept responsibility for our own acts because of the acute sense of inadequacy stemming from our low Self-Esteem. *Fault-finding*, that is, finding fault with another because he or she does not have or comply with our own particular values, stems from a need to compensate for our own self-condemnation, mistakes and feelings of inadequacy, guilt and feeling unworthy and "less than." Thus, we often vainly endeavor to make *ourselves "right"* by making *others "wrong."* We usually get the most upset with those who do the very things we heartily dislike in ourselves. In fact, we most often describe ourselves in our destructive criticism of others, for when we don't like something in ourselves, how can we allow others to get away with it? Our compulsive demand for *attention* and *approval* is caused by an intense need to be recognized and appreciated as worthy and lovable individuals, because we are unable to recognize and appreciate our own innate worth and importance, because of our need for validation as a worthwhile person. Our compulsive need for confirmation and agreement itself is caused by our desperate need to be "right" — to be accepted and approved.

Our aggressive *need to win*, our fierce competitive drives, spring from identification with our actions and the resulting desperate need to prove our individual worth and importance by our achievements — to be "better than" in order to boost our Self-Esteem. Our compulsive *need to overeat, to drink or smoke excessively*, usually results from a futile effort to satisfy a gnawing, insatiable hunger for self-approval and acceptance, as well as a need to compensate for the discomfort and hurting of self-rejection. *Depression* is largely caused by disgust and discouragement with ourselves and our inability, because of our sense of inadequacy and unworthiness, to achieve the success and happiness we feel we "should." *Divorce*, one of the most common and disruptive consequences of low Self-Esteem, is most often caused by the low Self-Esteem of one and usually of both partners; for low Self-Esteem manifests in excessive control, possessiveness and the resentment and bitterness caused by continual fault-finding and the generally inharmonious and destructive life style engendered by low Self-Esteem. Most of our emotional turmoil, in fact, is caused by a deep sense of insecurity and inadequacy plus a driving need to be recognized — to love and be loved. *Indecision* is usually a matter of being afraid to make a mistake, for with low Self-Esteem we cannot tolerate a mistake because of feeling or being considered less capable and effective than our peers.

Futility is mainly caused by our inability to make decisions and thus to function effectively, owing to a severe sense of inadequacy and dependency, to the fear of making a commitment, and to our almost total absorption in our own sense of inadequacy and the problems resulting therefrom. *Greed* and excessive *acquisitiveness* are mainly caused by our intense need to prove our worth — by a driving need for recognition and approval, for owing to our faulty conditioning and resulting low Self-Esteem we measure our personal worth by the wealth, power and prestige we can achieve over that of our peers. Gross *selfishness* also is caused primarily by our all-absorbing interest in our own needs and sense of inadequacy. Consequently, we have neither the time nor the inclination to recognize or be concerned with *other's* needs, desires and problems.

Hate often results from the fancied threat of someone whom we consider superior to ourselves. It also often originates from an effort to compensate for our hatred of self, the inner message being: "How can I not hate you when I hate myself?" *Hopelessness* results from excessively low Self-Esteem, from a conviction that we have neither the opportunity nor the ability to be loved and lovable, happy and successful because we feel inadequate and worthless. *Insecurity* itself is caused primarily by a terrible sense of inadequacy and unworthiness. *Jealousy* and *envy* are also symptoms of low Self-Esteem. When we feel inadequate, impoverished and too worthless to deserve the good things of life, it is very difficult to tolerate others having them.

Lack of close friends is almost entirely a matter of low Self-Esteem, for the two classic ways of handling low Self-Esteem are either fierce aggressiveness or almost complete withdrawal, neither of which attracts or keeps friends. Moreover, anyone suffering from low Self-Esteem is very critical, demanding and *value judging. Nothing* prevents or destroys friendships more than adverse value judgments. *Loneliness*, too, stems from low Self-Esteem, from an inability to feel warm and friendly toward ourselves and thus an inability to feel warm and friendly toward others. Furthermore, we cannot be comfortable alone with an individual self that we reject and despise. When we achieve sound Self-Esteem, we *enjoy* being alone with ourselves.

Masks and *barriers* are built when we feel inadequate, "less than" or worthless; we cannot stand to have others discover how truly worthless or unimportant we feel we really are. Thus, we wear masks and build barriers to keep people from seeing us as we "really are" and so close ourselves off from others — and from life. Our need to *dominate* and *control* stems from a need to achieve a sense of power and importance in a vain effort to gain self-approval. *Possessiveness* toward a friend or spouse springs from a need to hold on to what we have, since we feel too inadequate, insecure and unimportant to ever "win another." *Pride* and *arrogance* are cover-ups for low Self-Esteem.

Procrastination stems largely from our fear of making a mistake, our fear that we will not do as well as we "should." So we postpone the moment of truth as long as possible. Procrastination also is the consequence of our inability to resolve conflicting needs because we feel too inadequate and dependent to make decisions. *Resentment* and *bitterness* stem primarily from *value judging* —

from demanding that others honor our particular values because of a compulsive need for confirmation and agreement. These negative emotions come in when people do not do as *we* feel or think they "should." *Resistance* and *rebellion* arise from our inability to accept the authority of a power figure, for with low or crippling Self-Esteem we feel that "taking orders" detracts from our own personal worth and importance.

Self-indulgence most often results from an effort to compensate for our self-rejection and hurting, from feeling bad and at odds with ourselves, which all goes back to inadequate Self-Esteem. *Self-pity* usually stems from our inability to take conscious charge of our own lives. We feel that we are at the mercy of fate and the whims of our fellow men, and that nothing is fair or equitable. *Snobbishness* is another attempt to compensate for or disguise our low Self-Esteem. *Suicide* itself is most often committed in a desperate effort to escape from one's rejected and despised self, and the miseries and hurting resulting from such self-rejection. *Timidity* and *embarrassment* usually result from our feeling "less than" and vulnerable to others' authority, their adverse opinions and attitudes. We *feel* vulnerable to others only when we accept their personal worth and authority over our own. The truth is that *no one* is innately one iota more or less worthy, more or less important than another, regardless of others' possessions, status or achievements. *Withdrawal* occurs when we do not feel sufficiently worthy to occupy our rightful place in society. Furthermore, we can feel only as warm, kind and loving toward others as we feel toward ourselves. Moreover, others tend to accept us at *our* own evaluation, thus compounding the problem of withdrawal.

In short, if you are to enjoy satisfying emotional *and* physical well-being, you *MUST achieve* and *maintain* sound Self-Esteem. There is NOTHING more essential to a happy, healthy and productive life. The choice is *yours*.

Now, granted that low Self-Esteem is damaging and destructive to your personal happiness and well-being, what can you do about it? In other words, how can you achieve sound Self-Esteem? The first step is to correct your *faulty conditioning* by checking the validity of your existing concepts, values, assumptions and beliefs against *observable reality*, against how you *actually function*. For you can function harmoniously and effectively only to the degree that you are in alignment with reality, with the natural laws and forces of life.

The following concepts point the way to correcting your faulty conditioning — to achieving a more free, happy and joyful existence. First, however, it is essential to carefully check them against how and why we *act* as we do — in other words, to make sure that these concepts *actually are* "realities of human behavior."

1. Our Awareness (which is defined as the *CLARITY* with which we perceive and understand, both consciously and nonconsciously, *everything* that *affects our lives*) determines everything we do. Therefore, we *can do* only as well as our current Awareness *permits*. In other words, any fault in our behavior lies *not in us* but in our *faulty Awareness*, which is the *automatic* product of our heritage and *total* life experience, including our faulty conditioning.

2. At the *instant* of any decision, our Awareness is temporarily *fixed* or *frozen*, for during that instant all *input has ceased*. Consequently, at any given instant there is *one* and *only one* decision we can possibly make. Thus, we invariably do the *best* we can at the time, however beneficial or destructive the consequences may be.

3. We are *each responsible* for our own life and well-being, for we cannot possibly escape the impact of the consequences of everything we think, say and do, regardless of any handicapping conditions or circumstances.

4. Since we are inescapably responsible for our individual lives, we have the *innate authority* to do as *we ourselves see fit*. We must, however, pay *whatever price is demanded* for our acts and behavior.

5. There are only *wise* and *unwise* acts, for we can act only as wisely as our prevailing Awareness permits. Thus, "fair and unfair," "moral and immoral," "right and wrong," "good and evil" can be no more than descriptive terms for specific wise or unwise acts.

6. We *are not* our *actions*, for we are *that which acts*. Our actions are but the *means*, determined by our Awareness, for satisfying our dominant needs. Thus we can neither *prove* nor *disprove* our worth by our behavior or by our achievements or lack thereof.

7. *All* value judging, condemnation, guilt and remorse are *totally unfounded* since we are *not* our actions and since we *invariably* do the *best our current Awareness permits*.

8. "To know better" is not sufficient "to do better," when one has a conflicting *need* that outweighs his *value* or *desire* "to do better."

9. We cannot possibly achieve *sound Self-Esteem*, that is, genuine love of self, until we purge ourselves of *all* shame, guilt and remorse, and *totally refrain* from value judging ourselves or accepting the value judgments of others. For genuine love *IS total unconditional acceptance*.

10. We cannot be hurt by the attitudes and opinions of others when we realize that we are neither our *actions* nor our *Awareness* — that *we are* unique and precious beings, ever doing the *best* our current Awareness permits, ever growing in wisdom and love.

By investigating, accepting and integrating the above concepts, you can correct your faulty conditioning relative to your own and others' behavior. This will enable you to rid yourself of any accumulated shame, guilt and remorse and to refrain from further adverse value judging of self — the fundamental requirement for achieving sound Self-Esteem, since the basis of sound Self-Esteem is total, unconditional acceptance of yourself — despite your mistakes, real or fancied shortcomings, and human frailties. For love *IS total unconditional acceptance!* And as you stop value judging and begin loving *yourself*, you will *automatically* stop judging and begin loving *others*. And as you start loving others, they will start loving you, for everyone, regardless of appearances, is aching to love and be loved.

To maintain sound Self-Esteem it is necessary to accept your own innate authority, take active charge of your own life, and establish a life style that generates and nourishes sound Self-Esteem. The Barksdale Foundation's "Life Style Evaluation," No.70, provides a reliable guide as to how you are progressing in this endeavor. *Do not*, however, be impatient or judgmental of yourself if you do not feel you are making the progress you "should." Remember, you can establish and enjoy this way of life only to the degree that your current Awareness and Self-Esteem permit.

If you have any question as to your individual level of Self-Esteem, you can answer this question by evaluating your Self-Esteem on the "Barksdale Self-Esteem Index." If you experience a need or desire to impress others with your worth or importance, you can be sure you *do not*, as yet, have *sound Self-Esteem!*

If you are to enjoy inner peace and freedom, if you are to release your tremendous potential and experience the richness and joy of life that is your birthright, you must achieve and maintain sound Self-Esteem. You cannot lead a fully happy and satisfying life without it!

NOTE: Consider and keep this thought in mind: "There are NO *faulty people* — only people *WITH faulty Awareness!*"

"MAIN LINE" TO SOUND SELF-ESTEEM
(Basic Affirmations for your Daily Program)

If you will alert yourself to your value judging and make the following Affirmations a reality throughout your day, every day, you will soon achieve sound Self-Esteem, for sound Self-Esteem IS total unconditional acceptance.

I REALIZE THAT I AM NOT MY ACTIONS AND THAT EVERYTHING I HAVE EVER DONE HAS BEEN DICTATED BY MY PREVAILING AWARENESS. THUS ANY FAULT MUST LIE *NOT WITH ME*, BUT WITH MY LIMITED AND DISTORTED *AWARENESS*.

I REFRAIN FROM JUDGING MYSELF, FOR I REALIZE I *AM NOT* MY ACTIONS AND *KNOW* I INVARIABLY DO THE BEST MY CURRENT AWARENESS PERMITS.

If you purge yourself of guilt, stop all value judging, thoroughly understand and deeply sense the reality of each idea of the following Affirmations — and meaningfully affirm them at every opportunity throughout your day, every day, until they are constantly alive in your consciousness, you will achieve sound Self-Esteem with an absolute minimum of time and effort.

MASTER AFFIRMATIONS FOR SOUND SELF-ESTEEM

EVEN THOUGH OUR AWARENESS MAY DIFFER, NO ONE IN THE ENTIRE WORLD IS ONE IOTA MORE OR LESS WORTHY, MORE OR LESS IMPORTANT THAN MY OWN PRECIOUS SELF.

I LOVE AND CHERISH MY WONDERFUL SELF. I REALIZE THAT I AM *NOT* MY ACTIONS, THAT I *AM* A UNIQUE AND PRECIOUS BEING, RESPONSIBLE FOR MY OWN LIFE, EVER DOING THE BEST MY CURRENT AWARENESS PERMITS, EVER GROWING IN WISDOM AND LOVE.

If you discipline (motivate) yourself to make the following Action Statements a "way of life," you will eliminate confusion, conflict and frustration, achieve greater productivity and success, and generate and nourish sound Self-Esteem.

BASIC ACTION STATEMENTS FOR SOUND SELF-ESTEEM

I AM MY FINAL AUTHORITY AND IN FULL CHARGE OF MY *OWN* LIFE AND AFFAIRS — TOTALLY RESPONSIBLE FOR EVERYTHING I THINK, SAY AND DO.

I PLAN MY DAY, DO FIRST THINGS FIRST, PATIENTLY, ONE AT A TIME, AND DO NOT FRET ABOUT WHAT I HAVE YET TO DO.

The Acid Test: If you still have a need or desire to impress others, you do not yet have sound Self-Esteem.

AFFIRMING YOUR RIGHT TO BE LESS THAN PERFECT

EVEN THOUGH I CANNOT ESCAPE THE CONSEQUENCES, I ALLOW MYSELF THE FREEDOM TO OVERINDULGE, TO "GOOF OFF," TO MAKE MISTAKES, TO BE DEFEATED, TO FAIL — FREE OF RESISTANCE, SELF-ACCUSATION, SHAME, GUILT OR FEELING "LESS THAN."

AFFIRMATION FOR RELEASE OF INNER TURMOIL

KNOWING I AM NOT MY ACTIONS OR AWARENESS, I REALIZE I HAVE *NOTHING TO PROVE.* THUS I AM KIND AND GENTLE WITH MYSELF — *FREE* TO *DO* AND *BE* AS I MYSELF SEE FIT.

AFFIRMATION FOR RELEASE OF PRESSURE

I AM FREE OF PRESSURE AND FRUSTRATION, FOR I REALIZE THAT I CAN DO ONLY WHAT MY TIME AND MY CURRENT AWARENESS PERMIT.

AFFIRMATION FOR ACCEPTANCE

I KNOW THAT ALL MY PROBLEMS AND HURTING ARE AIDS TO MY NEEDED LEARNING AND GROWTH — TO THE EXPANSION OF MY AWARENESS — AND RESIST NOTHING I CANNOT CHANGE.

ACTION STATEMENT FOR SELF-DISCIPLINE

I DO NOT DRIFT OR PROCRASTINATE. I DISCIPLINE MYSELF THROUGH BEING AWARE OF WHAT IS OF PARAMOUNT IMPORTANCE IN MY LIFE AND GENER-ATE THE NECESSARY MOTIVATION TO BRING IT ABOUT.

ACTION STATEMENT FOR LOVING RELATIONSHIPS

I REFRAIN FROM ALL VALUE JUDGING, FOR EVEN THOUGH I MAY NOT LIKE WHAT OTHERS SAY OR DO, I CONCEDE THEM THE RIGHT TO THEIR OWN AWARENESS AND THUS AM FREE OF RESENTMENT, ANIMOSITY, BITTERNESS AND HATE.

AFFIRMATION FOR HUMILITY

I AM FREE OF PRIDE, FOR I REALIZE THAT HOWEVER EXEMPLARY MY CON-DUCT OR ACCOMPLISHMENTS MAY BE, I CAN DO ONLY WHAT MY CURRENT AWARENESS ENABLES ME TO DO.

AFFIRMATION FOR COMPASSION

I AM LOVING AND COMPASSIONATE TOWARD ALL WHO ARE HURTING BE-CAUSE OF THEIR UNWISE ACTIONS. I REALIZE THAT EXCEPT FOR *MY* MORE FORTUNATE AWARENESS I COULD BE THE ONE HURTING.

CHECK LIST
FOR
A FREE AND HAPPY LIFE

These are suggestions, not directives. However, the more you live in accord with them, the more happy, free and loving — the more successful you will be. In fact, if you conscientiously follow these suggestions, "shoulds," "oughts" and "musts" will cease to have meaning for you. For you will then *automatically* become a loving, caring individual, as much or more interested in the happiness and welfare of your fellow man as in your own — owing to your overflowing love, happiness and joy of living. *THE CHOICE IS YOURS!*

We suggest that you:

1. Investigate the value of these suggestions and conscientiously implement those which you accept as sound and meaningful. Give them top priority in your day-to-day living for they can revolutionize your attitudes and enjoyment of life.

2. Exercise your *innate* authority over your own life and recognize your responsibility for your own well-being. Do not miss out on life by default. Take *active* control of your life and keep it. Since you cannot possibly escape responsibility for your life and well-being, it is much better to make mistakes than to procrastinate or drift along the path of least resistance.

3. Recognize and correct your faulty conditioning regarding human behavior — determine what IS, *how* and *why* you actually function as you do. Internalize your revised concepts of behavior until you automatically act and react in alignment with them.

4. Stop being dependent on others. Exercise your own authority — make your own decisions. Stop seeking confirmation and agreement, authority and approval from others. No one has greater inner wisdom and strength than you. No one else knows better what is *best* for *you*.

5. Stop identifying with your actions and do not try to prove your worth by your achievements. Do not evaluate your worth through externals — through your appearance, possessions or status. Instead, recognize and accept your own *innate* value and importance.

6. Forgive yourself for all past mistakes, defeats and shortcomings, knowing you are not your actions and that you have invariably done the best you could at the time. Purge yourself of all condemnation, blame, shame, guilt and remorse, and refrain from any *further* self-accusation.

7. Motivate yourself to sound self-discipline by recognizing what is truly best for you, for both long and short range. Retain only positive self-audited thoughts, for self-discipline (controlled motivation) requires control of your thoughts, desires, images and expectations.

8. Realize that your every act is a response to a personal need and that your *dominant* need, conscious or nonconscious, inevitably determines your *every* act.

9. Be aware that you have the freedom, ability and *responsibility* to control your dominant needs by consciously determining what thoughts you allow to dwell in your mind. Examine the needs behind your motivation to make sure they are real and undistorted. Only by being aware of and controlling your needs can you effectively direct your life and assure your well-being.

10. Envision, anticipate and affirm only *desired* conditions and situations in your life and affairs, for *statements of being* — be they *negative* or *positive*, voiced or otherwise — have a subtle way of becoming actualities when empowered with imaging, feeling and expectations.

11. Accept the fact that you can do *anything you choose, anything at all* within your natural capabilities, by making and implementing a firm clear-cut decision, *provided* that you have no *conflicting* need strong enough to stop you.

12. Choose your goals and every day make some contribution, however small, towards accomplishment of these chosen objectives. Rejoice in even the slightest evidence of progress and be willing to live with a sense of incompletion.

13. Eliminate drifting, procrastination and self-indulgence from your life. Plan your work and activities and reduce all repetitive work to a daily routine. Make *"total"* decisions and do first things first, patiently, one at a time, and do not fret about what you have yet to do. This suggestion is a *"magic formula"* for precluding confusion, conflict and frustration.

14. Be willing to make a mistake, to be defeated or fail. Make your *own* decisions, the best you can make at the time, and be willing to accept the consequences, however unsatisfactory or destructive they prove to be.

15. Determine the reality of every undesired situation and face it honestly and fearlessly. *Recognize* and *accept* what IS! Resist nothing *you cannot change* and change forthwith that which you can. Resistance of reality causes more emotional turmoil and hurting than any human action, other than adverse value judgments of one's self.

16. Tension is caused by unfulfilled personal needs. Accept tension as a natural part of a living organism and learn to understand and live with it. Tensions are essentially "growing pains" and are often intensely painful. All tension is a demand or signal to act — to resolve your confusion, conflict or frustration — a signal to get comfortable with yourself, to grow in wisdom and love.

17. Treat grief as a natural release for a sense of loss. Realize that death is but a transition to another phase of learning and growth — as natural an incident to existence as birth — that self-pity, guilt and resistance only result from distortions of our Awareness.

18. Realize that good and evil, right and wrong, moral and immoral are but descriptive terms — that there are only wise and unwise acts as determined by the individual's or group's prevailing Awareness. Recognize that "sin" is but a mistake and "evil" its natural consequence — that all experience, both "right and wrong," "good and evil," are but stepping stones for our needed learning and growth — for the expansion of our individual Awareness.

19. Do not allow others' opinions and attitudes or your need for confirmation and approval cause you to feel hurt, "put down," insulted, rejected or inferior. You *are* absolutely invulnerable; however, you *CAN feel vulnerable* if you accept their Awareness and authority over your own. Remember, no one is more or less worthy, more or less important, than your own precious self.

20. Keep in mind that no two people have the same Awareness — that we are each motivated by different values, assumptions, beliefs, pressures, needs, goals and aspirations. Consequently, allow everyone the right and freedom of his/her individual Awareness and *STOP all value judgments* — of both *yourself* and others — now and *FOREVER.* For we each *have to do* what our individual Awareness *motivates us to do* at the time. You cannot possibly achieve sound Self-Esteem as long as you indulge in adversely judging yourself.

21. Convert any resentment, hate or bitterness to *compassion* through conscious realization that, regardless of the consequences, everyone is doing exactly what he/she *has to do* at the time, i.e., what his/ her current Awareness dictates.

22. Cherish and nourish your physical well-being. It is difficult to really *"feel good"* if you do not feel well and fit physically. Moreover, the best of intentions are useless if you do not have the health and energy to implement them.

23. Find sufficient time for your needed rest and relaxation or you will go stale. Excessive fatigue generates depression.

24. Conscientiously work on improving your Self-Esteem until you no longer value judge others or have a need to impress your friends and associates *or* strangers.

25. Determine *who you are* and work out a personally satisfying philosophy — something that will provide an anchor against the stresses of life.

26. Set aside adequate time for contemplation of "the true, the good and the beautiful" and for regular meditation on your relationship to your Source.

27. Forego all anxiety, fear and worry by the realization that the *real you* is intangible, that it cannot even be touched, let alone hurt or *separated* from its *Source.*

28. Above all, continually affirm:

I LOVE AND CHERISH MY WONDERFUL SELF, FOR I REALIZE THAT I AM *NOT* MY ACTIONS, THAT *I AM* A UNIQUE AND PRECIOUS BEING, RESPONSIBLE FOR MY OWN LIFE, EVER DOING THE BEST MY CURRENT AWARENESS PERMITS, EVER GROWING IN WISDOM AND LOVE

until these truths are *ever uppermost* in your consciousness.

NOTES

LOVE AND AN ACHING HEART

Several times at church I have heard the minister intone at the end of his service, "We must now all go out and *love* our *fellow men.*" I subscribed to this admonition but it always made me feel more worthless and guilty.

Why? Because, not having experienced real, genuine love, I didn't even know what love was — let alone how to go about loving my fellow men. Thus, his admonition only made me feel less worthy and more guilty for not being able to do what "the good book" said I "should." I assumed that I was the only one unable to do this. I took for granted that I loved my wife and family, since everyone is *expected* to. In retrospect, I realize that my "love" was more a matter of need and that I perceived them to be an extension of my own unworthy, crippled self and was possessive, harsh, controlling and critical. I know now that I was about as unloving of them as I was of my own inferior self. I made myself think I was knocking myself out working 12 to 15 hours a day, including Saturdays and Sundays, *for them* and *their* welfare. I now perceive that I was primarily trying to satisfy a desperate compulsive drive to prove my own personal worth — that my intense distorted need to succeed was often more meaningful to me than they or their welfare. I never knew a moment's peace.

The wonderful here and now was but a bridge of impatience, emotional turmoil and hurting, between regret, remorse and guilt for the past and anxiety for the future. The beautiful living present ever evaded and passed me by.

I concluded I was simply too selfish and egotistical to genuinely care for anyone, and rejected and loathed myself all the more. In a desperate effort to compensate, to gain a measure of self-approval, I knocked myself out trying to *"help others"* — to give my thirsting brother a drink from my own little jug, not realizing that it was empty — that there was nothing — no genuine help or caring. Thus, I became a frenetically busy "do-gooder" and a compulsive "people-pleaser." I built barriers and assumed many masks to avoid exposing my real self. Even though others considered me a great success, a "hail fellow well met" and an exemplary humanitarian, inside I was still no good, inadequate and fearful — in *desperate* need of *approval* and *acceptance.* I could not accept a genuine compliment, no matter how justified, for *I knew* that *I* was just no damn good and that the bestower was either stupid or trying to con me into something for his own ends.

Naturally, it never occurred to me that my basic problem was that *I didn't love myself,* for I had been conditioned to confuse self-love with egotism — that to love one's self is "bad." But even if I *had* realized I didn't love myself, I would not have had the slightest idea how to go about doing it.

Instead, I tried desperately to prove my worth so I could accept myself. Owing to my confused and distorted awareness, I somehow thought that, if I could get others to approve and look up to me, I would be okay. So I strove mightily to be a success — to accumulate wealth and prestige. And with this desperate, hurting, compulsive drive I did *"succeed."* I drove Fleetwood Cadillacs; I always bought the best and most expensive of everything. I had the biggest and best house in the neighborhood, the largest and most beautiful swimming pool, the most gorgeous landscaping and the most impressive view lot. I sent my kids to the "best" private schools. I was looked up to and admired. I never missed an opportunity to drop the names of my prominent, influential friends, to tell anybody and everybody what a tremendous individual I was — but, of course, in a clever and socially acceptable way — how I started from nothing and did it *all* on my own. I spent a ridiculous amount of time on local, state and national committees. I joined all the right clubs and was careful to be seen with all the right people. With this desperate hurting drive I built a highly successful international business, but still could not bear to really see myself in the mirror. I kept up with the Joneses — even surpassed them — with a vengeance. But it still didn't work. Such evidence of success, once gained, was as *dust in my mouth.* I still felt isolated, worthless and empty inside.

In my compulsive drive for success and approval, I generated such frequent and agonizing migrain headaches that for years I was practically an invalid. I had two severe cases of ulcers and such high blood pressure I often thought my head would explode.

But out of all my emptiness and hurting was generated an intense search for the answer. The breakthrough came when I suddenly realized that my basic problem was that I actually *hated myself.* Now that I had the problem pinned down, I could intelligently proceed to resolve it rather than simply hurting and stewing in my own juice.

I finally learned how to *love* myself, to be happy and joyful, and was astonished to learn that, despite their masks and barriers, despite their worldly success and approbation, that practically *everyone else* was suffering to a greater or lesser degree, with the same handicapping, hurting, if not indeed, *crippling* lack of Self-Esteem. It was *not,* after all, just me who was "no damn good" — who was empty and hurting inside.

Finally, in my painful, unending search for self-acceptance — in my intense probing, checking and cross-checking, here is what I was able to discover. That no one need prove his/her worth; that we are all innately worthy; that *no one* is one iota more or less worthy, more or less important than another. I learned that one does not *need* the compulsive, hurting drive generated by lack of Self-Esteem to succeed, that we have a *natural* urge to grow, to express and fulfill ourselves — that we can grow, blossom and bring forth fruit just as does a plant or a tree, because *that is our nature.*

I discovered that we *are not our actions;* that our actions are but the *means* we select to *fulfill our dominant need* and that, thus, we cannot prove our worth by our achievements. I learned that we can act only as wisely as our awareness permits. That we are each invariably doing the absolute *best* we can possibly do at the time, for at the instant of decision, our awareness is fixed or frozen. I thus discovered that all self-accusation, condemnation, shame, guilt and remorse are *totally* unfounded. And that all we have to do to genuinely *love ourselves* is to *stop all adverse value judgments of ourselves.* And that, as we do this, we *automatically stop* value judging *others.*

Above all, instead of actually hating my brother as I hated myself, I now *love my brother* — each and every one — with *an overflowing love that is warm and wonderful,* that makes me feel really good inside. In other words, I learned how to *love my neighbor as myself* — for love IS *total unconditional acceptance* — and it *has to START with YOURSELF! And* all my physical problems *automatically* disappeared.

So, if you want more friends — true friends, if you want more loving relationships with your spouse, children, parents — with *everyone* with whom you come in contact — if you want *sound* Self-Esteem, if you want to release your fantastic potential, in short, if you want to truly *LOVE YOUR FELLOW MEN* — *STOP value judging yourself* — NOW, *totally* and *forevermore!*

HOW TO LOVE THY NEIGHBOR AS THYSELF

The minister who closes his service with, "We must now all go out and love our fellow men," generates a deep sense of inferiority and guilt in those who have not experienced genuine love — that is, love as total unconditional acceptance. Those who experience "love" as possessiveness and control, who suffer from self-rejection and self-hate, more commonly "*hate* their neighbor as they hate themselves." And the tragedy is that they do not know *how*, nor does anyone — including their minister — tell them *how* to love others.

But there is a way — a very simple and foolproof way to genuine, meaningful love both for yourself *and* your fellow man. No one, of course, needs to be *taught* to love — for the *ability* to love is a universal gift. The problem is to remove the impassable roadblock to loving erected by your faulty conditioning and resulting distorted Awareness. For the purpose of this article, Awareness is defined as the *clarity* with which we perceive, both consciously and nonconsciously, *everything* that affects our lives. As such, it is the *automatic* product of our heredity, intuition and total life conditioning up to the present instant.

We can love ourselves, and others, *only* to the degree that we can perceive and integrate the fact that "there are NO faulty *people* — that there are only people with faulty *Awareness.*" For the basis of genuine, unselfish, undistorted love *IS* total, unconditional acceptance. Thus, we can love only to the degree that we believe that every individual is a unique and precious being — that we refrain from all adverse value judging both in our hearts and in our attitudes and actions — to the degree that we refrain from ALL fault-finding, all accusation and condemnation, both of *ourselves* and of others.

Now, just what do we mean by value judging? Value judging is the assignment of praise or, more commonly, condemnation to a person for his conduct, endeavors, personal characteristics, life style, etc. It is based on the assumption that the other individual has the same Awareness, and therefore, the same concepts, ideals, needs and values that we have. In other words, adverse value judging or fault-finding is a criticism of yourself or others for doing or not doing something that violates your own particular set of values. It manifests itself in unfounded "oughts," "musts" and "shoulds" and is the most harmful and destructive action in which we can indulge relative to our Self-Esteem and personal relationships, for it precludes or actually *destroys* love.

But how can *you* stop value judging? You have been conditioned to indulge in value judging from the instant you were born — by your parents, by your playmates, teachers, ministers, friends, associates, in fact, by everyone with whom you have come in contact — in other words, by a lifetime of faulty conditioning.

It is apparent, therefore, that if you are to stop value judging, you must first correct your faulty conditioning. You must get your thinking and behavior into alignment with reality — with what actually *IS*.

But how? By checking your concepts, values, beliefs and assumptions against *observable* reality — by carefully and deeply probing for the causes of everything you think, say and do — especially your motivations and the needs which generated them — especially your attitudes and emotional reactions.

Fortunately, such intense, careful probing has already been done, has been carefully checked and rechecked over a period of some 30 years by the writer and those he has worked with. They are listed here for your personal observation and investigation. Now, if you can check their validity, if you can apprehend their truth with clarity and deep understanding, if you can internalize them so that you *automatically* act and react in accord with them, then — and only then — can you love your neighbor as *yourself*. Why? Because you can then accept and love *yourself*. And once you can totally and unconditionally accept yourself, that is, can be completely free of all adverse value judging, then — and only then — can you accept and love your neighbor in like degree.

Deeply understanding and *living* the following concepts is the most crucially important endeavor you can possibly undertake, for genuine love of self (that is, *sound* Self-Esteem) is absolutely essential to fulfillment of your fantastic potential — to a rich and meaningful existence, a life of purpose and contribution — to your happiness and joyful well-being.

The more you question and check the following statements, the more meaningful and helpful will they become, for the more they will then be *yours* — the more deeply convinced you will be there are NO faulty *people*, only people with faulty *Awareness* — with *faulty conditioning!*

OBSERVABLE REALITIES OF HUMAN BEHAVIOR

Explanatory Note: As we use the term, Awareness is the *clarity* with which we preceive, both consciously and nonconsciously, *everything* that affects our lives. As such, it is the *automatic* product of our individual heritage and total life experience, including our *intuition*.

1. Every human act is an attempt to satisfy a *personal need.* Thus our *actions,* good or bad, are but the *means* we choose to fulfill our dominant needs.

2. Our basic need is to *"feel good"* about ourselves — mentally, physically and emotionally.

3. Our basic and *ultimate* motivation is to do what *we most want* to do, that is, *what we would rather do than not do* — what we *think* will make us "feel good."

4. The choice *is always ours,* but it is inevitably based on what we *think* will make us feel best under the circumstances — on what we would rather do than not do at the *instant of decision.*

5. We can do *only* what our *needs motivate* us to do. Our Awareness is responsible for both our *needs* and *how* we fulfill them, for it presents us with the data that determines what we would rather do than not do. Thus, our individual Awareness, *in effect,* determines, or *"dictates,"* everything we do, or do not do.

6. A *price* is exacted for our every act. Such price is determined by the requirements and unwanted consequences of the act. Other than for spontaneous or compulsive actions, our specific motivation is determined by weighing our needs against the costs of the alternative *means* of satisfying them.

7. We mistakenly do things against our own self-interest — things that are hurtful to ourselves and/or others because of our faulty Awareness, our *distorted needs* and/or the *unwise means* we choose to satisfy our needs.

8. We are each *unique* in that no two individuals can have the same Awareness, exactly the same heritage and total life experience. Thus all personal comparisons are *invalid*, for we each have different concepts, aspirations, values, needs and pressures motivating us.

9. There are only *wise* and *unwise* acts, for we can act only as wisely as our prevailing Awareness permits. Thus, "fair and unfair," "moral and immoral," "right and wrong," "good and evil" can be no more than descriptive terms for specific wise or unwise acts.

10. At the *instant of any decision*, our Awareness is temporarily fixed or frozen, for during such time *all input has ceased*. Consequently, at any given instant there is *one* and *only one* decision we can make. Thus, we invariably do the *best* we possibly can at the time, however beneficial *or* destructive the consequences may be.

11. We are *each* inevitably *responsible* for our *own life and well-being*. We cannot possibly escape the impact of the consequences of everything we think, say and do, regardless of any handicapping conditions or circumstances.

12. Since we are inescapably responsible for our individual lives, we have the *innate* authority to discharge that responsibility — that is, to do *as we ourselves see fit*. We must, however, pay the price exacted by the consequences of our every act.

13. We are *not* our *Awareness*, for we are that which is *aware*. Neither are we our *actions*, for we are that which *acts* — our actions are but the means we choose to fulfill our needs. We cannot, therefore, *prove* or *disprove* our personal worth by our achievements or lack thereof.

14. Since we are *not* our *actions* or *Awareness*, all value judging, *praise* and *blame*, condemnation, guilt and remorse are *totally* unfounded. Likewise, there is no rational basis for reward or punishment. Any "reward" lies in the "feel good" of *initiating* wise and constructive acts, and any "punishment" lies in the "feel bad" of *having initiated* unwise and destructive acts.

15. "To know better" is not sufficient "to do better," when we have a conflicting *need* that outweighs our value or desire "to *do better.*" Furthermore, there is no such thing as a "weak will" or a "sheer act of will," for both terms merely denote the particular individual's *degree* of *motivation*.

16. It is not what happens to us but how we handle it — our reactions and attitudes, our *acceptance* or *resistance*, our Awareness of reality — that determines our *"feel good"* or *"feel bad."*

17. We cannot possibly achieve *sound Self-Esteem*, genuine love of self, until we purge ourselves of *all* shame, guilt and remorse and totally refrain from judging *ourselves*, for genuine love *IS total unconditional acceptance*. As we stop value judging *ourselves*, we *automatically stop* value judging *others* and are then both *loving* and *loved*.

18. Everything we think, say and do is a manifestation of our individual Awareness. No one is more or less worthy, more or less important than another, for we are *all equal*, all *innately* worthy and important, varying only in our level of Awareness. Any fault lies *not in us* but in *our faulty Awareness*.

19. The only obstacle to our inner peace and freedom, happiness and joyful well-being is our limited and distorted Awareness. Lack of Self-Esteem itself results from a *distorted* Awareness of the *realities of human behavior*.

20. Since our fundamental need is to *feel good* about *ourselves*, genuine *success* is fulfillment of that need, that is, the achievement and maintenance of *sound Self-Esteem*. With sound Self-Esteem all doors are open.

Recommended Exercise for Loving Both Yourself and Others

Once you fully realize that — even though you do not have to *like* your own or others' values or actions — that ALL value judgments are totally unfounded — pick a day and keep count of *every time* you judge yourself. Also count the times you judge others throughout the day. You will find that the more often and meaningfully you affirm: I LOVE AND CHERISH MY WONDERFUL SELF, FOR I REALIZE THAT I AM *NOT* MY ACTIONS — THAT I *AM* A UNIQUE AND PRECIOUS BEING, RESPONSIBLE FOR MY OWN LIFE, EVER DOING THE BEST MY CURRENT AWARENESS PERMITS, EVER GROWING IN WISDOM AND LOVE, the easier it will be for you to stop judging yourself. Count the number of your self-judgments for a full day, once or twice a week, until *you stop judging yourself altogether.* You will find at this point that you have also stopped judging *others,* and that you feel JUST FINE — for you will now be *LOVING YOURSELF!* Refraining from all value judging will take a bit of doing at first, but it can be done and there is absolutely nothing that will pay greater dividends to YOU — especially in Self-Esteem and in relations with your spouse, mother-in-law and children — to say nothing of your "boss," co-workers and, if you have them, customers or clients!

REMINDER: Refraining from value judging, from all critical "shoulds," "oughts" and "musts" is the most vitally important action you can possibly take for *achieving sound Self-Esteem.* But such action must come from the heart — from a deep understanding that simply discontinuing to verbalize value judgments will not do the job, for mental reservations and nonverbal communications are realities. To be effective, you must stop value judging yourself, *both* consciously and *nonconsciously,* because *you realize* that *ALL* value judgments are totally unfounded and ridiculous — that *everyone,* including yourself, must inevitably do what he or she *has to do* at the time, however good, bad or indifferent that action may be. To stop value judging because of a moral admonition or simply because *we say so* will have little or no impact on you or on your interpersonal relationships. Never forget that you can love others *only* to the degree that you *stop judging* and *start loving YOURSELF!*

When you do start loving others, you will find that they start loving you — they can't help it! Stopping all value judgments works — it REALLY WORKS! And why not? Because *Love IS unconditional acceptance,* whether it be of yourself or of others. If you want to love and to be loved, simply *stop value judging NOW — totally and forever!*

STOP RESISTING AND START LIVING

Resisting unwanted realities we cannot change causes more human misery than anything we can do — and we do it to *ourselves.* We can be happy and at peace with ourselves only to the degree that we recognize and *accept* reality. If you really want to hurt, just resist something you cannot change. You will inevitably succeed in such endeavor, for it is not what happens to you that causes your hurting, but how much you resist its unwanted reality.

Now here are some questions for your consideration:

We talk a lot about reality. What exactly do we mean? Reality is something that IS and cannot be changed, at least at the time of reference. While a given reality *IS* the *same* for EVERYONE, our individual PERCEPTION of a reality may be quite different, depending on the CLARITY of our individual Awareness.

What do we mean by personal reality? Some characteristic of a person — mental, physical or emotional — that is an actual fact and that neither the person nor anyone else can change, even though the given reality may exist for only an instant. It might, for instance, be a certain individual's Awareness, the color of his skin or the length of his hair.

Now, are a person's concepts and values a reality? Yes, they certainly are — just as much as having only one leg is a reality for a one-legged man.

Why are one's values a reality? Because they *are* and cannot be *changed* at any given instant. They stem from a person's Awareness, and at any given instant they are as fixed and frozen as a cake of ice! They are as much the individual's reality as is his blue eyes or his physical body.

Now, what causes practically ALL emotional hurting and accentuates all physical pain? Resistance! Resistance to your own or to another's personal reality, or the reality of a situation or condition that you cannot change.

Now just what is resistance? Resistance is the refusal or inability to allow a reality to *just be* — to walk away and simply *let it be,* just as you let light and dark or the mountains and the sea BE. For what is, IS, whether you like it or not.

What is the source of resistance? Resistance stems from the *baseless* assumption that *you* are somehow entitled to anything you WANT and/or to ACCEPTANCE by others of your own individual values, concepts, beliefs and assumptions. In other words, it is the false and destructive *assumption* that we do not have to tolerate anything we do NOT like that generates futile and hurtful resistance.

Now what is the evidence of resistance to another, or to his actions? Value judging and being unable to accept the reality that the other person must comply with his own needs, values, beliefs and assumptions and *cannot* therefore comply with your particular concepts and values. And they are *never* alike, for no two people have the same *total* life experience and intuitional insights generating their concepts and values.

How can you *stop* resisting reality? By *conscious* recognition of the particular reality and a deep understanding that it cannot be helped or changed at the time. In short, by allowing the other individual the right and freedom of his own individual Awareness, however limited or distorted his Awareness may be — *and* allowing *yourself* the freedom to accept that particular behavior and *LET IT BE,* without feeling a need to "straighten out" the other individual or his concepts and values.

What is the prerequisite for doing this? You can do this to the degree, and only to the degree, that your current level of Self-Esteem permits. If you are still value judging *yourself,* you will continue to criticize and condemn *others* and to resist their reality — their Awareness that spawned their concepts, values AND their undesirable actions. For how can you be easy on others when you are so harsh and demanding of yourself! The truth is, you can allow others the right and freedom of THEIR Awareness ONLY to the degree that you can allow YOUR-SELF the *right and freedom* of YOUR Awareness!

What is another crucial factor that makes it so difficult to stop resisting reality? Even though you *may* recognize the reality of the person or the situation, you have little chance of ceasing to resist it *unless* you are *aware* that you are resisting. Very few people, indeed, are conscious of their resistance and thus unable to stop their resistance.

Now here are some examples of resistance: Self-pity results from resisting a condition you strongly dislike and/or feel is "unfair." There is nothing more destructive to your emotional well-being than sitting on the "pity-pot."

The dying of a loved one. You resist the reality of the person's dying because of a sense of guilt or you do not feel you can bear the loss, or you feel a threat to your emotional and/or physical security. In short, because you are emotionally and/or physically dependent on the loved one.

You make a mistake at work and your boss is hard on you. You are value judging him for undesirable behavior and resisting his value that you shouldn't make mistakes. Specifically, you are resisting the fact that he did not comply with *your* value that a boss should be sweet and kind, even though you *did* make a mistake.

Another example: Suppose your mother had a very limited and distorted Awareness. As a result she rejected you, gave you a very difficult time and a faulty and inadequate preparation for life. But although you *understand* that she could not help it, for you realize that she always did do the best her prevailing Awareness permitted, you still bear her intense animosity and bitterness.

Why? You still have a NEED for a "good mother" and are RESISTING the reality that your mother was incapable of being a "good mother" because of her limited and distorted Awareness. In short, you never *accepted* the reality that she *was* UNABLE to comply with your concept or value of how a "GOOD MOTHER" *"should"* act.

Is it not apparent from these examples that it isn't what happens to you but *the degree that you resist the reality* of the particular person or situation that causes you pain and suffering? Although you do not have to like it, acceptance of the particular reality of each of the foregoing examples would have alleviated the pain, hurting and resentment.

Now some more questions for your consideration: Why do you allow rudeness, obscenity or profanity to "bug" you? Because of your inability to accept the reality of another's values and thus allow him the right and freedom of his own Awareness — because of your adverse value judgment and *resistance* to the particular individual's values — because he does not act or speak as *your* values demand he "should."

What causes practically all human relations problems such as resentment, anger, hostility, hate, bitterness, jealousy and envy? Inability to allow the other individual the right and freedom of his own Awareness and *then* value judging and *resisting* his particular values which are, of course, different from your own, owing to his different environment and total life experience.

Now, what causes more heartache than practically any one thing? What causes so much resentment, hostility and alienation between parent and offspring, between in-laws? Adverse value judgments and *resistance to each other's values.*

Now what are the most common symptoms of resisting? "Oughts," "shoulds," "musts," "it isn't fair," etc.

Why does a person get his dignity or feelings hurt? He really doesn't, he only thinks he does, for one's hurting is caused by his resistance to threat or injury to his own concepts and values by what the other person says or does.

Consider how can an individual possibly be hurt when he is an intangible essence — when he cannot even be located, let alone touched or hurt.

Hurt feelings are a misnomer — there are only injured concepts and values. You feel "put down" and "less than" when you do not receive the confirmation and support you wanted because you gave the other party the authority to be right over *yourself*. You simply cannot be hurt emotionally when you allow both *yourself* and others the right and freedom of your individual Awareness.

What is the *ultimate* in resistance? Suicide! Resistance to a life you have judged to be untenable.

Some other examples of resistance:

ENVY is resistance to the reality that another has personal characteristics or possessions you feel are more desirable than your own.

JEALOUSY is resistance to a threat to your emotional well-being.

WORRY is resistance to some threatening event or situation that you fear *might* happen and is normally based on a sense of inadequacy and/or dependency.

HATE is resentment and resistance toward one who threatens your emotional and/or physical well-being.

FRUSTRATION is resistance to the reality that you can do ONLY what your time, energy and prevailing Awareness permit.

DIVORCE is caused by resistance to and refusal to tolerate your spouse's individual Awareness — his or her values, concepts, assumptions and beliefs.

What is an important conclusion you can draw from the foregoing discussion? That in the final analysis it is not the value judging of other people, itself, that is so emotionally upsetting and destructive — it is *resistance* to the *values* and to *those who hold them!*

Resistance is pushing a person from you, while acceptance is drawing him to you — that is, rejection vs. love.

BUT you *do not* have to *approve* the other's values or actions in order to accept him as a desirable and *lovable individual*. Neither do you have to tolerate his actions if they are actually interfering with your own personal well-being.

What is a crucially important fact about resistance? That if you are hurting, you are *resisting* some unwanted reality. If you want to stop hurting, find out what it is you are resisting and, if you cannot change it, agree to *let it be!* Just as you let the sun, moon and stars BE.

What is the one and ONLY thing that keeps you from "feeling good" ALL the time? You can feel only as good as your prevailing Awareness permits. With sufficient Awareness you would: 1.) be living more wisely and harmoniously, and 2.) not resist anything you could not change.

What must absolutely happen in order for you to feel angry, resentful or bitter toward another? You adversely value judge the other for not complying with your own particular values and then *resist* both him and his values. In other words, you refuse to allow him the reality — the right and freedom of his own individual Awareness, even though you realize he has his *own* concepts, values and beliefs and thus cannot possibly do otherwise.

Hostility, resentment, anger, hate and bitterness are but a few of the destructive emotions stemming from *resistance*. For how can you possibly generate such emotions *without* resisting another's Awareness? What you are *really* resisting is the particular individual and his needs and values, *and* how he satisfies them, which neither you *nor* the individual can possibly change *without* a change in his Awareness?

What can we conclude from the foregoing? That it is not what *happens to us* that causes our emotional turmoil and hurting but *the degree that we resist* it — especially the reality of others' Awareness.

While we may not like what another does, we would resist neither him nor his actions if we had a "gut level" understanding that, despite the unwanted consequences, one can do ONLY what his Awareness determines *"he would rather do than not do"* under the circumstances.

Thus we can conclude that resisting what we do not like or want is as futile and witless as starving to death in the midst of plenty — as foolish and futile as resisting the sunrise or sunset! Just remember that it is the RESISTANCE — *not* the unwanted reality — that basically causes your emotional turmoil and hurting.

The choice is always YOURS — as are ALSO the *consequences!*

...make friends with life...

PRAISE VS. RECOGNITION AND APPRECIATION

Praise implies and reinforces the concept that if you are not a "winner" you are a "loser" — a reject on the scrap heap of broken hopes and aspirations. The purpose of this article is to point out the destructiveness of praise and to suggest a valid alternative that is not destructive to your Self-Esteem.

It is quite important, in order to minimize any resistance, that this article be recognized as a presentation of ideas rather than a demand for confirmation and agreement — ideas that we perceive to be of tremendous importance to both the individual and to society. Since the term "Awareness" is of prime significance, it is well to define what we mean by this term. Awareness, as we use the term, is the clarity with which you perceive and understand, both consciously and non-consciously, *everything that affects your life.* As such, Awareness is the automatic product of your individual heredity, your intuitive insights and your total environmental conditioning. You will no doubt perceive that, as such, your Awareness is responsible for all your concepts, values and assumptions, beliefs and ideals. Consequently, it either generates or makes you cognizant of all your needs, pressures and attitudes. Thus it actually determines your every decision and choice, your every action and reaction. In fact, your Awareness is responsible for *all* your behavior.

Now, before we can make an intelligent presentation, there must be agreement, at least temporarily, on the meaning of some other relevant terms. Otherwise it would be like two ships passing in the night, for we would be unable to achieve a meeting of minds on what we mean and thus get nowhere.

For our immediate purposes, therefore, we define these terms as follows:

REALITY: The kind of reality we refer to is *observable* reality — what you can individually perceive to be self-evident or rationally true. For example, the law of gravity, the rising and setting of the sun; your needs, values, pressures and emotions; how and why you behave as you do, etc.

NEEDS: A need is a desire so strong that it must be fulfilled or resolved if you are to "feel good" physically and/or emotionally. Your needs may be authentic, false or distorted; instinctive, intuitive or generated by your conscious Awareness.

VALUES: A value is a characteristic, concept or material thing of relative importance to an individual and/or society. Your values may be sound, false or distorted.

ACTIONS: Your action is but the *means* you choose to fulfill your dominant needs. You are not your actions, for you are that which acts. Your every choice and action are determined by the data presented by your prevailing Awareness.

CREDIT: Credit is a favorable value judgment — an expression of commendation — of glorifying and honoring and mentally assigning an increment of worth to an individual because you consider he performed in an exemplary manner, or because he possesses admirable characteristics arising from his self-generated causation.

PRAISE: Praise is the assignment of credit for a "praiseworthy act," that is, an act that complies with your particular system of values.

VALUE JUDGMENTS: Value judging is the assignment of praise or, more commonly, condemnation to a person for his conduct, endeavors, personal characteristics, life style, etc. It is essentially based on the assumption that the other individual has the same Awareness, and therefore the same concepts, ideals, needs and values as you. In other words, value judging is a criticism of yourself or others for doing or not doing something that violates your own particular set of values. It manifests in unfounded "oughts," "musts," "shoulds" and "should nots."

Now, we perceive praise to be an invalid and destructive value judgment. Since your prevailing Awareness determines what you have to do at any given instant, there is no rational justification for either praise or credit. No matter how exemplary or "praiseworthy" your act, you could not, with your prevailing Awareness, have acted otherwise.

Thus the fundamental reason praise is destructive is that it is out of alignment with reality. And you can be harmonious, happy and at peace with yourself only to the degree that you function in alignment with reality — with what actually IS!

Probably the most destructive characteristic of praise is that it identifies or locks you in with your actions. For, since praise says you are good because of your "good" acts, conversely it says you are bad anytime you make a mistake or act "bad." Thus you are conditioned to self-accusation, shame, guilt and remorse every time you act or behave less than "perfect." But, thoughtful consideration of how anyone actually functions as an individual discloses that there are no faulty or "bad" people, that there are only people with faulty Awareness.

Another destructive consequence of identifying with your actions is that you must prove or validate your worth by your conduct and achievements. This concept ignores the reality that your very existence proves your innate worth and importance in the scheme of things — that you are inherently a unique and precious being, ever doing the best your current Awareness permits and ever growing in Awareness — in wisdom and love.

Furthermore, when you feel you have to validate yourself by your performance you raise a very disturbing question: "When have I done well enough?" This question has no satisfying answer to one who is hooked up with his actions and dependent on praise for a sense of personal worth. In fact, it is the trying to do "well enough" that is at the root of the need to do or be "better than," which, in turn, is the cause of greed, envy, jealousy, aggression and gross selfishness.

The fact that praise is normally based on comparison with the actions, personal characteristics, possessions or prestige of others makes it even more destructive. For no matter how hard you try to excel, to be the "best" or "better than" in any given area, you can always find others who have done "better" — have made more money, have a finer home, more prestige, or what have you. Thus, it is always a "no win" game which generates guilt and a sense of inadequacy. You can never do "well enough" while equating personal worth with your acts or accomplishments because there is never a cut-off point — never anything to tell you when you have done "well enough." Also, you realize at some level that comparisons do not count because they are invalid. For you know that no one else has the same Awareness — the same heredity and total conditioning, the same intuition as you — thus everyone has different concepts, assumptions, beliefs, values and capabilities, different understanding, needs and pressures inhibiting or motivating them. Thus, what another does or does not do has no rational bearing on what you do or do not do.

Praise ignores or invalidates one's inherent worth and importance and implies that one must prove his worth, that is, validate himself through others' approval of his conduct and accomplishments. This desperate need for approval and validation is the basic cause of gross selfishness. How, for example, can you take the time to care or be concerned about the problems and needs of others when you have such an intense, driving need to justify your very existence? Thus, identification with your actions and your need to "be better than," which is implied and fostered by praise, is the actual cause of envy and jealousy, fierce competition, overriding aggression, and ultimately of war itself. Identification with one's actions is the basis of all reward and punishment, condemnation, shame, guilt and remorse. It is responsible for adulation on the one hand and capital punishment on the other.

Praise contributes to lack of Self-Esteem, for it implies and validates blame. If you are subject to praise for good acts, you are, *per se,* subject to blame for bad behavior or inferior accomplishments. You are thereby tied into self-accusation, condemnation, shame, guilt and remorse, which make sound Self-Esteem impossible, for sound Self-Esteem is based on genuine love of self, and genuine love of self requires total unconditional acceptance of self.

Furthermore, how can you possibly avoid feeling "less than," inadequate or worthless every time you make a mistake or turn in an inferior performance when you are conditioned by way of praise, to blame and belittle yourself for non-acceptable or inferior acts or achievements — for not doing as well as you "should," based on your own or other's standards? And how can you take the time and effort to be concerned, loving and caring toward others when you are so absorbed in self-blame, guilt and remorse because of your mistakes, shortcomings and human frailties, especially when you have an overpowering need for acceptance, approval and praise in order to feel your life is worthwhile?

Praise, with its implication of condemnation and blame for unwise actions, inhibits and fosters withdrawal in one whose Self-Esteem is so low he does not feel he can risk condemnation or feeling "less than" for his possible mistakes and failures.

Praise also generates a sense of dependency. If you are so conditioned that you must receive praise in order to "feel good," how are you going to feel when you are not receiving praise?

Even without all its damaging and destructive effects, praise would not build Self-Esteem, because: 1) at some level you realize that praise and comparisons are invalid; 2) if you have low or inadequate Self-Esteem, which is almost universal in our destructive value-judging culture, you are unable to accept praise because *you* know you are inferior or "no damn good." Thus, anyone who praises you is either "stupid" or trying to con you into something for his own ends; and 3) no matter how exemplary your actions, you can always observe someone else doing significantly better.

Moreover, praise and its ugly twin, blame, like reward and punishment (which are equally unfounded), are very manipulative and coercive in personal relationships, especially with low Self-Esteem individuals.

Now that we have looked at the destructive effects and implications of praise, let us look at a procedure that acknowledges your innate worth and constructive actions, free of praise with all its destructive connotations — a valid alternative for helping you to "feel good" about yourself that encourages or motivates you to act constructively and harmoniously because it is in alignment with reality.

This procedure is the simple recognition of a constructive and desirable act and non-judgmental appreciation of its consequences. In other words, instead of a value-loaded comment or compliment, it is simply a factual observation of an act that provides sound and desirable benefits — benefits that are sound because they are in alignment with reality. It is based on the realization that you can do only what your prevailing Awareness dictates, however "good" or beneficial the consequences may be. It is, in fact, nothing more or less than recognition and appreciation of another's Awareness, or, if applicable, of your own. Such an observation is conducive to a healthy self-satisfaction, free of all pride or egotism. In short, the self-satisfaction that stems from conscious realization that you are fulfilling your innate urge to grow and express because it is your nature to grow and express — free of comparison or any distorted sense of being "better than."

While the actual words for recognition and appreciation may be similar or even identical to those of praise, the tone of voice and body language are distinctly different because the former are totally free of any emotionally loaded value judgment. You will find that most people, especially children and young people, respond more favorably to simple recognition and appreciation of their constructive acts than they do to praise, for they sense that they are being acknowledged as individuals instead of being evaluated on the basis of their actions — that they are unique and worthy regardless of their conduct, actions or human frailties.

Thus, if you want to function in alignment with reality and contribute to the well-being of others, refrain from praise. Instead, extend simple recognition and genuine appreciation for a job well done.

VITAL FACTS OF HUMAN BEHAVIOR

1. Every human act is a response to a personal need. Thus, you cannot change a given behavior without first changing the motivating need.

2. You have an INNATE need to fulfill your potential just as an apple tree has a need to blossom and bring forth apples.

3. It is not what happens to you but how you handle it — your attitudes, reactions and choices — that determines your "feel good" or "feel bad."

4. If you are harsh and demanding of others, you are harsh and demanding of yourself.

5. If you have a need to *impress others,* you have not yet achieved sound Self-Esteem.

6. If you are "hurting," you are *resisting* some reality.

7. If you are not happy and at peace with yourself, you are still *value judging* yourself.

8. If you are still *value judging* yourself, you are still identifying with your actions and your Awareness.

9. If you cannot allow *others* the right and freedom of their own individual Awareness, you are critical and judgmental of them because you are still blaming and condemning *yourself* — because YOU are *not* allowing YOURSELF the right and freedom of YOUR Awareness.

10. You cannot be harsh, selfish, mean and unloving toward others if you truly love yourself.

11. If you feel *vulnerable* to the attitudes and opinions of others, you do not yet have sound Self-Esteem, for you are denying YOUR innate worth and authority.

12. You neither CAN nor NEED prove your worth and importance by your behavior or achievements.

13. ALL praise and blame, condemnation and guilt, reward and punishment are TOTALLY invalid.

14. If you are experiencing difficulty in achieving sound Self-Esteem, you are still *value judging yourself,* probably on a *non-conscious level.*

At ALL costs, be *constantly* AWARE:

1. You are neither *your ACTIONS nor your AWARENESS.*

2. You can do ONLY what you would *rather* do than NOT do.

3. You are *inevitably* doing the BEST your current Awareness permits.

4. You are a *UNIQUE* and *PRECIOUS being,* ever growing in wisdom and love.

5. NO ONE in the ENTIRE world is one iota more or less WORTHY, more or less IMPORTANT, than your own precious self.

6. No one NEED or CAN validate YOU, for you are INNATELY a unique and precious being.

7. Any FAULT in your behavior lies not in YOU but in your *FAULTY Awareness!*

ESSENTIAL REQUIREMENTS FOR BUILDING SOUND SELF-ESTEEM
(Roadmap to Sound Self-Esteem)

Maintain an Awareness of the crucially important benefits of Sound Self-Esteem and give building Sound Self-Esteem TOP PRIORITY in your life for the short time required to achieve it.

Recognize and exercise your own *innate* authority to do what you yourself see fit (see paper No. 13, "I Am My Own Authority") and take *conscious* charge of your own life. That is, be the *final authority* for everything you think, say and do. Make and implement your own decisions and commitments. Do not drift or vacillate — *any* decision is better than no decision at all.

Stop value judging and resisting any unwanted Realities. If you *cannot,* or choose NOT to *change* them, *accept* and *allow* them *to be,* just as you let daylight and dark BE.

If you are to achieve sound Self-Esteem you must absolutely STOP *ALL* value judging, for the fundamental *basis* of sound Self-Esteem IS *genuine love of self*, and this entails TOTAL *unconditional acceptance* of *yourself.* This means you must be completely free of any and ALL *value judging* — from all self-condemnation, shame, blame, guilt and remorse. In other words, if you are to achieve sound Self-Esteem, you must:

1. STOP *ALL* adverse value judging and *resisting* of *yourself*

2. STOP *ACCEPTING* the adverse value judgments of *others*

3. PURGE *YOURSELF* of ALL condemnation — of all shame, blame, guilt and remorse.

However, you can stop value judging and resisting yourself and others ONLY to the degree that your prevailing level of Self-Esteem permits. On the other hand, value judging, either conscious or non-conscious, drastically diminishes or destroys your *existing* Self-Esteem. The only way out of this dilemma is to *use your affirmations on a daily basis*, preferably as recommended in your Daily Schedule. Please note: *There is NO other way.* Thus IF you are in dead earnest about achieving Sound Self-Esteem, you literally *must* use the appropriate affirmations — either the pre-recorded affirmations tapes *or* as a *structured meditation.* In either case, sense the meaning and impact of *every* word and phrase as you repeat your chosen affirmations.

What has to happen to ENABLE *you* to DO this? You must fulfill these FOUR *essential* requirements:

1. Get your *conscious* Awareness in *alignment with Reality.* TOTALLY convince yourself of the validity of the Laws and Realities of Human Behavior. Conscientiously use your Pocket Companion during every available sliver of time — DO NOT procrastinate!

2. Get your *non-conscious* Awareness into *alignment with Reality.* Internalize the Realities of Human Behavior through using your affirmation tapes per the Daily Schedule. Also use your "Main Line to Sound Self-Esteem" and other miscellaneous affirmations. Integrating your affirmations at a non-conscious level is absolutely *essential* to achieving sound Self-Esteem. Otherwise, you will continue to value judge yourself at a *non-conscious level* and not even be aware that you are thereby negating your efforts toward achieving sound Self-Esteem.

3. *Establish* and *maintain* a life style that is in *alignment with Reality*. Implementing the "Life Style for Sound Self-Esteem," is an essential requirement for building and maintaining sound Self-Esteem.

4. Have a personal philosophy that is in *alignment with Reality*. If you do not now have such, it is of vital importance that you DO work one out that is MEANINGFUL and satisfying to YOU.

ABOVE ALL, BE AWARE:

I AM AS *WORTHY* AND *IMPORTANT* AS ANYONE ELSE IN THE *ENTIRE WORLD*. I AM ALL RIGHT, *TOTALLY BLAMELESS*, JUST AS I AM. I, MYSELF, CANNOT POSSIBLY *BE ANY BETTER*, FOR *ONLY* MY AWARENESS CAN BE IMPROVED.

CAUTION! If you are to achieve Sound Self-Esteem it is *essential* that you do *NOT* value-judge and resist yourself for *value judging and resisting yourself.* For you can do ONLY what your prevailing level of Awareness and Self-Esteem *enable you to do.*

110

THE REALITIES OF MY EXISTENCE

THE LAW OF HUMAN BEHAVIOR

Despite moral values, obligations, circumstances or the consequences, *one can do only what he most wants to do — what he would rather do than not do* — what he thinks will make him feel *best* in the prevailing situation, for his fundamental need is to *"FEEL GOOD,"* mentally, physically and emotionally.

COROLLARY TO THE LAW OF HUMAN BEHAVIOR

One can act only as wisely as his prevailing Awareness permits, for his Awareness — the CLARITY of his perception and understanding — determines what he would rather do than not do. Thus, if one is to change his behavior, he must have new input to his Awareness in order to change his dominant need or the means chosen to satisfy it.

THE TEN BASIC REALITIES OF MY BEHAVIOR

1. My very existence proves my innate worth and importance. No one in the entire world is one iota more or less worthy, more or less important than my own unique and precious self. Therefore, NO ONE CAN *validate* me or *prove my worth.*

2. I am inescapably responsible for *EVERYTHING I think, say, do and FEEL,* for I inevitably benefit or suffer according to the consequences of my actions. Thus, if I do not "feel good," it is my responsibility to determine the cause and either eliminate it or choose to ACCEPT its *effects.*

3. Since I AM inescapably responsible — that is, *answerable* — for my own life and well-being, I have the *innate* authority to fulfill that responsibility. Thus, I have the right and freedom, within my inherent and physical capabilities, to do *ANYTHING I myself* see fit — *anything at all!*

4. I am NOT my Awareness — I am that which is aware. (I certainly am not the CLARITY of my perception and understanding.) I am entitled to neither credit *nor* blame for my Awareness, for at any given instant it simply is what it IS — the *automatic* product of my heredity, my intuitional insights and my *total* life experience.

5. I am NOT my actions — I am that which acts. Thus, I am not "bad" if I act "bad." My actions are simply the MEANS I choose to fulfill my dominant needs. Moreover, since I am not my actions, I can neither prove nor disprove my worth by my achievements or lack thereof.

6. I must pay a PRICE, as determined by the *TOTAL consequences* of my act, for *EVERYTHING* I do or do *NOT* do. Hence, if I am to act *wisely,* I must first accurately anticipate and evaluate the *TOTAL price* demanded for my proposed action or inaction, and then deliberately determine *whether or not* I am *able* and *willing* to pay such price.

7. It is not what happens in my life that determines my *"feel good"* or *"feel bad,"* but how well I *recognize* and *handle* the *REALITIES* involved and, in particular, how well I *ACCEPT* any *unwanted realities I CANNOT CHANGE.* For I can stop "hurting" only to the degree that I *STOP RESISTING* them.

8. I am *NOT to blame* for any personal inadequacies, mistakes, defeats or failures, for I am not my actions and can act only as wisely as my prevailing Awareness permits. Since it is my Awareness that determines *what I would rather do than not do,* any fault in my behavior or endeavors lies NOT in me but in my limited or distorted Awareness.

9. Despite any unacceptable actions, I am alright *just as I AM* and am entitled to love and compassion *rather* than to condemnation, resentment, hate or bitterness.

10. The ONE thing I must do IF I am to achieve sound Self-Esteem, and thereby enjoy the tremendous *"FEEL GOOD"* it generates is to STOP VALUE JUDGING *myself*, both consciously and *non-consciously.*

AFFIRMATIONS OF THE REALITIES OF MY EXISTENCE

1. I realize that, regardless of the consequences, I can do ONLY what I would rather do than not do.

2. I am aware that I can act ONLY as "good" or wisely as my prevailing Awareness permits.

3. I perceive that my VERY EXISTENCE proves my INNATE worth and importance.

4. I recognize that I am inescapably responsible for EVERYTHING I think, say, do and FEEL.

5. I realize that I have the right and freedom to do ANYTHING I choose.

6. I know that I am NOT my Awareness and I refuse to accept blame for any mistakes, defeats or failures.

7. I realize that since I am not my actions, I cannot prove my worth by my achievements.

8. I perceive that I must inevitably pay the price demanded for everything I do.

9. I recognize that it is not what happens to me that determines my "feel good" or "feel bad" but how I handle it.

10. I realize that I am NEVER to blame for my actions, even though I *am* inescapably *responsible* for EVERYTHING I think, say, do and FEEL.

11. I now perceive that, regardless of any faulty behavior, I am alright JUST AS I AM and I am entitled to love and compassion rather than to condemnation, resentment, hate or bitterness.

12. I realize that the ONE thing I must do to achieve sound Self-Esteem is to stop value judging, now, TOTALLY and forever!

HOW TO "FEEL GOOD"

To "FEEL GOOD," I need to have a meaningful purpose (meaningful to me) and to take time to "smell the flowers" along the way as I pursue that purpose.

I CANNOT "feel good" living in the PAST or FUTURE and experiencing GUILT and RESISTANCE in the present.

It is my personal responsibility to "feel good." If I do not, it is because I do not choose to do what is REQUIRED to "feel good."

Every morning I ask myself: "Do I feel good?"

If I "feel bad," it is because I am value judging and resisting an unwanted reality, for I realize that there is NO other way to hurt emotionally. (Worry, anxiety and fear are but my resistance to what I think MIGHT happen — I do it ALL in my head.)

If I am to "FEEL GOOD," I must be my own authority and accept full responsibility for my own life and well-being. I therefore CHOOSE to fulfill the following REQUIREMENTS for "feeling good."

FIRST, I must be deeply aware of the vital significance of the following five Realities to be able to STOP VALUE JUDGING, to preclude self-accusation, guilt and resistance. Furthermore, if I am to be totally free of VALUE JUDGING and thus of resentment, anger, hostility and bitterness — and I certainly CANNOT "FEEL GOOD" unless I AM FREE of these destructive emotions — I must realize that the following Realities apply EQUALLY to my spouse, children, relatives, friends and associates, and allow EVERYONE the RIGHT and FREEDOM of his or her OWN UNIQUE AWARENESS.

1. MY VERY EXISTENCE PROVES MY INNATE WORTH AND IMPORTANCE. NO ONE in the entire world is ONE IOTA more or less worthy, more or less important than my own unique and precious self.

2. I AM NEITHER MY ACTIONS NOR MY AWARENESS. I am not my actions — I am that which acts. My actions are simply the MEANS I choose to satisfy my NEEDS. Neither am I my Awareness — I am that which is aware. My Awareness is simply the CLARITY with which I perceive and understand, both consciously and NON-CONSCIOUSLY, EVERYTHING that affects my life.

3. I CAN DO ONLY WHAT I WOULD RATHER DO THAN NOT DO. Therefore, despite the consequences and despite any admonitions or accusations to the contrary, I can do only WHAT MY TIME, ENERGY AND CURRENT AWARENESS PERMIT, for it is my Awareness that determines WHAT I WOULD RATHER DO THAN NOT DO. Thus, I am totally free of frustration and self-recrimination and thereby am able to manifest my tremendous innate potential for constructive and productive work.

Should I do something I regret, it is because I have acted unwisely. If I am to be free of regret, I must accurately determine both the benefit and the required price of a proposed act, and THEN decide if I am willing and able to pay it.

4. I AM *NEVER* TO BLAME. Any fault in my BEHAVIOR or ENDEAV-ORS lies not in me but in my LIMITED or FAULTY AWARENESS. For it is my prevailing Awareness that DETERMINES my EVERY CHOICE and DECISION, since it is my Awareness that decides what I WOULD RATHER DO THAN NOT DO. If my Awareness is distorted, both my NEEDS and my ACTIONS — the MEANS I choose to satisfy them — are apt to be out of alignment with Reality — out of harmony with WHAT IS.

   (a) I am NOT bad if I act "bad" or make mistakes, for I am NOT my ACTIONS.

   (b) I am NOT bad if I act "bad" or make mistakes, for I am NOT my AWARENESS, and it is my Awareness that determines EVERY-THING I think, say, do and feel.

   (c) I am NOT bad if I act "bad" or make mistakes, for I am not to blame for a faulty Awareness, since at any given instant my Awareness simply is WHAT IT IS — the AUTOMATIC product of my HERED-ITY, my INTUITIONAL INSIGHTS, and my TOTAL LIFE EX-PERIENCE.

5. I CANNOT CHANGE ANY UNWANTED REALITY BY LABELING IT "BAD" AND RESISTING IT. If I am to "feel good," I must RECOGNIZE any unwanted reality I cannot change and forego all value judging and resistance. I must simply "let it BE," just as I let the mountain and trees BE.

SECOND, I must absolutely refuse to indulge in value judging and self-accu-sation — to accept or harbor any shame, blame, guilt or remorse on either the conscious or NON-CONSCIOUS level.

THIRD, I must anticipate and visualize the total consequences of any doubt-ful action I am TEMPTED to take. Then, imagining I have taken such action, I must ask myself, "How did it make me feel?" — "Would I have felt BETTER had I NOT taken this action?" If I am to "feel good," I must then be guided by my answers.

FOURTH, I must willingly accept any UNWANTED REALITY I cannot change and simply LET IT BE! When faced with any problem, I must ask myself, "What is the REALITY of this situation?" — and THEN proceed accordingly.

The ULTIMATE requirement for me to "FEEL GOOD" is to achieve sound Self-Esteem, for I can STOP value judging and resisting ONLY to the degree that my existing level of Self-Esteem permits. And I can achieve sound Self-Esteem only to the degree that I internalize the following affirmation on BOTH the conscious and NON-CONSCIOUS level:

I AM ALL RIGHT, TOTALLY BLAMELESS, JUST AS I AM. I, MYSELF, CANNOT POSSIBLY BE ANY BETTER, FOR ANY FAULT IN MY BEHAV-IOR OR ENDEAVORS LIES NOT IN ME BUT IN MY PREVAILING AND EVER EXPANDING AWARENESS, FOR WHICH I AM SUBJECT TO NEI-THER BLAME NOR CREDIT. ONLY MY AWARENESS CAN BE IMPROVED.

OBSERVABLE REALITY
of Human Behavior

You are not your Awareness — you are that which is Aware. Your Awareness is the CLARITY with which you perceive and understand, both consciously and non-consciously, EVERYTHING that affects your life. You are entitled to neither credit nor blame for your Awareness since it is the automatic product of your heredity, your intuitional insights and TOTAL life experience — and at any given instant it simply is what it IS, frozen in space and time.

You can do only what your Awareness indicates you would rather do than not do, for your ultimate need is to "feel good." Therefore, you invariably do what you THINK will make you feel BEST under the prevailing circumstances. Thus, you can act only as "good" or wisely as your prevailing Awareness permits.

You are not your actions — you are that which acts. Your actions are but the means, as determined by your prevailing Awareness, to satisfy your dominant needs. Consequently, you cannot prove your worth by your achievements. By the same token, mistakes, defeats and failures cannot make you unworthy or "less than."

Now since your Awareness determines EVERYTHING you do and since you are NOT your Awareness, any fault in your behavior or endeavors lies NOT in you but in your limited or distorted Awareness. Thus, you are never to blame or subject to shame or embarrassment for your actions, no matter how unacceptable or destructive the consequences may be.

Nevertheless, you ARE responsible for EVERYTHING you do, for you cannot possibly avoid the consequences, no matter how "good," "bad" or indifferent they may be — in other words, aside from any benefits, you can never escape paying whatever price is demanded for your actions. Thus, like it or not, you ARE in charge of your own life, and inescapably responsible for your own well-being. The choice is EVER yours — and ALSO the CONSEQUENCES!

IMPLIED REALITIES OF HUMAN BEHAVIOR

1. All value judging of myself or others is totally unjustified, for we are not our actions and we can do only what our Awareness causes us to most want to do.

2. All personal comparisons are unjustified as a measure of my performance or personal worth, for no one else has the same Awareness — the same drives, pressures, talents and capabilities I have.

3. Within my inherent and physical capabilities, I can do anything I want — but what I want is determined by my prevailing Awareness.

4. I invariably do what I "have to do," for I can do only what my prevailing Awareness indicates will make me feel best under the existing circumstances.

5. I unfailingly do the best I can at the time, regardless of the consequences, for I can do only what my prevailing Awareness motivates me to do, what it indicates *I would rather do than not do.*

6. Regardless of how exemplary my actions, I am entitled to neither credit nor praise, for I can do only what my prevailing Awareness enables me to do.

7. A price is inevitably exacted for everything I do. Such price consists of the demands and unwanted consequences of the act, such as any time, energy or money expended plus my having to forego alternative endeavors.

8. In spite of any adverse or handicapping circumstances, I am in charge of my own life and well-being, for I benefit or suffer according to everything I think, say, do and FEEL.

9. Everything I do, I do because I "want to," even though such motivation is generated by my unwillingness to pay the price demanded for not doing it. In other words, I would "feel worse" if I did NOT do it.

10. Regardless of my needs and desires, I can do only what my time, energy and prevailing Awareness permit — that is, what I would rather do than not do at the time. Even though this may be termed "procrastination" or "laziness," it is impossible to do otherwise without additional input from my intuition or personal experience.

11. To "know better" is not sufficient for me to "do better" when I have a conflicting need that outweighs my desire to "do better."

12. There is no valid justification for reward or punishment, for I can do only what my prevailing Awareness MOTIVATES me to do. Any "reward" lies in the "feel good" of initiating wise and constructive acts, and any "punishment" lies in the "feel bad" of having initiated unwise and destructive acts.

13. A limited and distorted Awareness generates both distorted needs and distorted means of fulfilling them.

14. "Right" and "wrong," "moral" and "immoral," "good" and "bad," "fair" and "unfair" can be no more than descriptive terms for my wise or unwise acts, for I am not my actions and invariably act as wisely as my prevailing Awareness permits. Therefore, I am not "bad" if I *act* "bad."

15. Even though what I do may be a big mistake, very destructive, unfair or immoral, and even though I may not approve of it, I can do only what I would rather do than not do — regardless of the consequences or what others may think, say or do.

16. I am invulnerable to others' opinions and remarks, for no one has greater power or authority over my life and affairs than I, myself.

17. At the instant of any decision, my Awareness is fixed or frozen and there is one and only one decision I can make, for during that infinitesimal point in time all input has ceased.

18. Everything I think, say, do and feel is a manifestation of my level of Awareness.

19. At any given instant I am exactly where my constantly changing Awareness has caused me to be. Just as a river can rise no higher than its source, I can do no better than my prevailing Awareness permits.

20. Both myself and others have the right and freedom of our own individual Awareness, regardless of how wisely or unwisely it motivates us to act.

21. Although I need not like or approve another's actions, I cannot get angry, bitter or resentful toward him if I realize he is not his actions and allow him the right and freedom of his own individual Awareness.

22. I cannot consciously expand my Awareness unless my prevailing Awareness motivates me to do so. Otherwise, my growth in Awareness is limited to the often hurting cause-and-effect relationships of my environment.

23. I am unique, for no two people have the same Awareness — the same heredity, intuitional insights and total life experience.

24. I have the right and freedom to overindulge, to "goof off," to make mistakes, to be defeated, to fail — free of self-accusation, shame, guilt or remorse.

25. My feelings stem from my concepts, values, beliefs and assumptions. If someone causes me to hurt, I am resisting his actions and the concepts, values, beliefs or assumptions from which they stem.

26. All my problems, turmoil and hurting are needed motivators for my learning and growth — for the expansion of my Awareness.

27. Practically all my emotional hurting is caused by my resistance to Reality, for I am harmonious and happy only to the degree that I accept and am in alignment with Reality.

28. If I am to discipline myself in line with my chosen objectives, I must control my thoughts, images, actions and reactions accordingly.

29. I cannot achieve sound Self-Esteem until I purge myself of all shame, blame, guilt and remorse and stop value judging myself.

30. Genuine success is "feeling good," for the ultimate motivation for everything I do is to "feel good," mentally, physically and emotionally.

31. I can be harmonious and happy, free and at peace with myself only to the degree that I am in alignment with Reality.

32. The only obstacle to my genuine success is my limited Awareness, for it is my Awareness that determines my alignment with Reality — that determines *"what I would rather do than not do."*

SELF-DISCOVERY

Life IS a "ball," but if you want to dance, get your feet out of the mud. It's okay to have your feet in the mud, but you can't dance that way.

If I am judgmental, harsh and demanding with OTHERS — *especially* with my loved ones (who, I know, will let me get away with it) — it is because, and ONLY because, I am NOT "feeling good" about MYSELF — because I am not consciously aware of the REALITY that I AM "OK" as IS! There is NO *other* reason — NONE whatever! For I know that *YOU are not your actions*, and that *you ARE invariably doing the BEST* your prevailing Awareness permits — that any fault or problem lies *not* in YOU but *in your Awareness*, for which *you* are entitled to *neither* BLAME *nor* CREDIT. It just IS. I *know*, therefore, that I am but trying to compensate for my own sense of being "unworthy, guilty or less than." Thus, if I am not "feeling good," the problem (and it *is MY problem*) is that I need to get my Awareness into alignment with *reality* — to realize at a *deep* level of my consciousness that I AM a UNIQUE and PRECIOUS being, *ever* doing the BEST my *prevailing* Awareness *permits*, *ever* growing in WISDOM and LOVE, regardless of my actions and their consequences.

If I am to "feel good," I must fully ACCEPT the fact that I do NOT have to be "better" or "better than" — that I AM *OK* the way I AM — that I AL-WAYS *have been and always will be* — that I CANNOT *help* being so — for any fault in my *behavior* or *endeavors* lies NOT in ME but IN my lack of Aware-ness. I KNOW that there is NO ONE in the *entire* world ONE IOTA more or less *worthy*, more or less *important* than my own *precious* self — regardless of what I DO or do NOT do, *or* of the resulting CONSEQUENCES.

If, however, I am to "feel good," I must be ever AWARE that even though I *can NEVER* help doing *"what I would rather do than not do,"* I *cannot* possibly *escape the consequences*. Therefore, if I am to be *happy and at peace with myself* — if I am to *FEEL GOOD* — I must acknowledge responsibility for my own life and be fully aware of *both* the potential benefits *and* COSTS of the proposed action, so that *"WHAT I would rather do than not do"* IS in alignment with reality — IS a *wise and constructive ACT*.

119

THE REALITY OF MY BEHAVIOR

I have my own individual Awareness, the *automatic* product of my heredity, my total life experience and intuitional insights.

I am fully responsible for my own life and affairs, for I cannot possibly escape the consequences of any act that affects my life, since I benefit or suffer according to the consequences.

I AM, therefore, *my own authority*, for I have the right and freedom to express my own individual Awareness — to freely determine the consequences of my every act. For it is my life and I cannot possibly escape the consequences of *anything* I think, say, do or feel. I am actually *in charge* of and totally responsible for my own life and well-being, whether or not I know it — whether or not I consciously accept or resist, even though I endeavor to escape that responsibility. For what is, IS — whether or not I *believe* or *accept* it. I can, however, be happy and free *only* to the degree that I recognize and wisely fulfill that responsibility. And knowing that, regardless of the consequences, I can think and DO *only* what my prevailing Awareness causes me to *rather do than NOT do*, I am TOTALLY free of self-accusation, shame, *guilt* and remorse. For I AM *invariably* doing the BEST I CAN possibly DO at the time.

MISCELLANEOUS AFFIRMATIONS

I am *inescapably responsible* for EVERYTHING I think, say, do and *feel*, for I *inevitably* benefit or suffer according to the consequences.

I willingly accept full responsibility for my own life and well-being and act accordingly.

I am neither my actions nor my Awareness and can act ONLY as wisely and harmoniously as my prevailing Awareness permits.

I allow myself the *right and freedom* of my prevailing Awareness and am *totally free* of self-accusation, shame, guilt and remorse.

I *am never to blame*, for any fault in my behavior or endeavors lies *not in me* but in my limited or distorted *Awareness.*

I am free of resistance and resentment, for I *CHOOSE* to do what *I have to do* and resist *nothing* I cannot change.

I am free of *frustration*, for I realize I can do ONLY what my *time, energy* and *prevailing Awareness* permit.

I do *first things first*, patiently, one at a time, and *do not resist or fret about* what I have yet to do.

It is not what happens in my life but how I handle it that determines my "feel good" or "feel bad" — my emotional turmoil or peace of mind.

I feel warm and loving toward my own wonderful self, for I am a unique and precious being, ever doing the best my prevailing Awareness permits, every growing in Awareness and love.

BECOMING YOUR OWN PERSON

It is very difficult being your own person when you have so many strings pulling you in so many different directions — strings pulled by family, friends, co-workers, aquaintances, etc.

What gives these strings so much power? Is it not *your* need for approval? *Your* need to be a "good kid"? Or perhaps *your* reluctance to hurt their feelings?

Now what is the problem in getting free of all this pulling and hauling? Is it not simply a matter of your being willing to pay the required price to cut these strings in order to gain the freedom to be yourself?

And what makes you so reluctant or fearful of paying this price? Is it not your lack of sound Self-Esteem?

The problem is definitely yours, for you *can* cut these strings any time you want. No one is likely to get their feelings hurt, or to not like you, if you are totally frank and honest with them — and if they do, is that not their problem? If they did get their feelings hurt, how long would it last? And how much more would they respect you for meeting your *own* needs and for being frank and honest with them? Might you not be contributing to their weakness and to your mutual dependency if you do NOT break these bonds?

Why does cutting these strings seem to entail such a grave risk? Is it not *your* distorted need for their approval — a need for them to accept and like you because of *your* own lack of SELF-acceptance and SELF-approval?

Take a hard look at these strings and their pulling power and see what you come up with, for you may not even be aware of these pulling strings unless you really *do* look for them. And, of course, you cannot cut them if you do not know they exist.

Is not *your* fundamental responsibility *your own* physical and *emotional* well-being — your own personal freedom and independence? How can you want and deliberately choose to help your fellowman if you do not "feel good" within yourself — if you are too involved in emotional turmoil and compulsive actions to choose freely?

Do you see how we trap ourselves with our emotional needs and false concepts? How we fool ourselves into thinking we are slaves to others' demands?

Of course, if you are aware of such strings but are in complete control of them, you need not cut them to be free.

But you ARE FREE to cut them if you CHOOSE!

DIRECTIONS VS. GOALS

You go life's way; life does not go your way when you are swimming against or across the current. When you are in alignment with reality — with what IS, life cooperates with you beautifully. When you do not, life bruises or perhaps even *breaks* you.

You cannot *force* life to go *your* way, for it inexorably goes *its own way*. It's fine to choose the direction you want to go — to choose your objective or purpose — but when you specify just *how* and *when* that purpose is to be fulfilled, you are going to get into deep trouble if you do not have the wisdom to chart a course that is in full alignment with the laws and forces of life.

For instance, if you set goals and deadlines, if you have rigid, unswerving expectations, you are going to get extremely disappointed and frustrated. Rigid expectations and deadlines not only lead to disappointment and frustration, but they project and *lock you into the future*, to "when your ship comes in." Goals and deadlines keep you from enjoying the rich and wonderful "here and now" — the ONLY *living time there is.* For the past is forever gone and the future has not yet arrived — and by the time it becomes the present you have already projected yourself into a new future — with your new, "bigger and better" goals. And thus you continually fail to experience the depth and fullness of the here and now. You become worn and old, your countenance wrinkled with the tension of trying to make life go according to your expectations and demands. And some morning you will wake up — if indeed you waken at all — and complain bitterly about what life has done to you.

Your children have grown and fled, your spouse is sick or dead, and still you are waiting desperately for your "ship of happiness," which continues to elude you because you keep it forever in the future. On the other hand, if you simply determine the *direction* you want to go — if you merely choose what you want to do with your life, and then let your awareness carry you forward with its own pattern and speed — patiently doing what is indicated, first things first, one at a time and not concerning yourself with what is yet to do — if you find the freedom to be at peace with a sense of incompletion — if you accept and enjoy life *as it comes* — not resisting or demanding it go *your* way, you will enjoy to the fullest the tremendous richness and wonder of the eternal present, joyous and thankful for what IS. And you won't then awaken sometime from your dream of the future and bitterly. ask to know "Why did life do this to ME?"

There is *still time* to replace the empty and barren "then and there" with the rich and fruitful "here and now." The choice is yours! You *can* yet experience the "NOW" by making an agreement with yourself to live in the *present* and let the future take care of itself — as it surely will, and harmoniously too, if you consistently do first things first without straining to meet your own *puny goals* and *expectations* — without *resisting* life as IT *"lives YOU!"*

If you want to go somewhere, climb on the right bus and just stay there. The bus will get you to your destination, for that is its job. Life is a game, and it's fun. If you want to catch the gold ring on the merry-go-round, simply "let go" and just "BE" — the ring will come around.

REALITY: REQUISITE FOR HAPPINESS

I am entitled to FEEL GOOD, for I perceive that inner freedom, peace and happiness are my birthright, and that I have but to free myself from the bondage of my faulty conditioning to claim it. Thus, my predominant need and responsibility is to achieve an Awareness that is in alignment with reality.

(1) I have a *choice* — I can be happy or unhappy. Thus, I do *not resist* any unwanted realities I cannot change, for I realize it is not the unwanted happenings in my life but the degree to which I resist them that causes my emotional turmoil, hurting and "feel bad." I realize that if I am hurting, I am resisting something I do not like or want.

(2) I have no need to be *validated* or to prove myself, for my very existence proves my inborn worth and importance, and there is *no one* in the entire world one iota more or less worthy, more or less important than my own precious self.

(3) I am in charge of my own life and well-being and am inescapably responsible for everything I do, for I inevitably benefit or suffer according to the consequences of everything I think, say, do and feel, and have the *innate right and freedom* to determine those consequences.

(4) I have total freedom, for even though I must pay the price demanded, I can do *anything I want* (within my inherent and physical capablities), but what I *want* is determined by my prevailing Awareness.

(5) I am not "bad" if I act "bad" — I am not unworthy or "less than" if I make mistakes, for *I am not my actions* and thus can neither prove nor disprove my worth by my achievements or lack thereof. *I am* the *non-physical essence* which acts. My actions are simply the *means*, determined by my prevailing Awareness, to satisfy my dominant need.

(6) *I am not my Awareness* — I am that non-physical essence which is aware, and can do only what my prevailing Awareness determines I *would rather do than not do*. Thus, I can act only as "good" or wisely as my prevailing Awareness permits.

(7) I am entitled to neither *praise* nor *recrimination*, for I can do *only* what my prevailing Awareness *enables* me to do. I am subject to neither praise *nor* blame for my Awareness, for it is the *automatic* product of my heredity, intuitional insights and *total* life experience and at any given time it simply is what it IS.

(8) I am totally free of all self-recrimination, impatience, pressure, conflict and frustration, for I realize that I can do only what my *time, energy and prevailing Awareness* permit. Thus, I do first things first, patiently, one at a time, and do not fret about what I have yet to do.

(9) If I am fault-finding, harsh and demanding with others, especially my loved ones, it is because I am fault-finding, harsh and demanding with *myself* — because my Self-Esteem has slipped.

(10) I do not judge myself, *resist*, feel inadequate, unworthy or "less than" when I make a mistake, for I realize that I can do only what my prevailing Awareness *enables* me to do and that my mistakes provide a major opportunity for getting my Awareness into alignment with reality.

(11) I am totally free of all self-condemnation and value judging — of all shame, blame, guilt and remorse, for I allow myself the innate right and freedom of my own unique Awareness.

(12) I am totally invulnerable to the attitudes, opinions, put downs and adverse judgements of others, for I realize that I unfailingly do the *best* my prevailing Awareness permits and accept no one's power or authority over my own.

(13) I am deserving of loving compassion, rather than condemnation, resentment, anger, hate or bitterness for my mistakes and unacceptable or hurtful acts, for I can do ONLY what my prevailing Awareness motivates me to do.

(14) I cannot possibly find fault or get upset with others if I *realize* they are neither their *actions nor Awareness* and *allow them* the innate right and freedom of their own unique Awareness.

(15) I am *alright*, totally *faultless, just as I am*, for any fault in my behavior or endeavors lies not in me but *in my prevailing Awareness.*

THE KEY TO EFFECTIVE COMMUNICATION
AND HARMONIOUS RELATIONSHIPS

You cannot possibly get emotionally upset, angry, resentful or bitter towards another individual, regardless of his opinions, attitude or actions, IF you recognize and acknowledge:

1.   That he is NOT his actions or Awareness — that he IS *separate* and *distinct* from both his actions and Awareness — that, thus, he is NOT "bad" if he acts "bad."

2.   The REALITY of his unique Awareness and accept his INNATE right and freedom to express that Awareness as he, himself, sees fit.

3.   That his values, pressures, needs, concepts, beliefs and assumptions *are REALITY* and accept the *fact* that he literally HAS TO DO what his prevailing Awareness indicates *he would rather do than not do* at the time.

4.   That all value judging is totally irrational and do not VALUE JUDGE and *RESIST* either *him* or what *he thinks, says, does or feels*, for this is the REALITY of his PREVAILING Awareness and cannot possibly be changed at any given instant.

5.   That any fault in his behavior or endeavors lies NOT in HIM but IN his PREVAILING Awareness.

This does not mean that you necessarily like or agree with his characteristics or values. It simply means that you accept them as the REALITY they actually are, *and* let them BE — just as you let the sun, moon and stars BE. Neither does it mean you *have* to condone or TOLERATE the other's undesirable BEHAVIOR. Not being emotionally upset, however, enables you to deal with any problem in the relationship calmly and intelligently, free of emotional distortion, resentment and resistance.

Be aware that value judging is, in effect, telling the other that he *should* have a *different* Awareness. This *is*, of course, *impossible*, since one's Awareness is the *automatic* product of his heredity, total life experience, *and* intuitional insights — *NONE of which* he can control at any given time.

ESSENTIALS FOR A HAPPY AND FULFILLING MARRIAGE

In reviewing the following requirements for a happy and fulfilling marriage, it is important that you be aware that a limited or distorted Awareness merely *explains* WHY a person acts in a distorted or destructive manner. It does NOT *excuse* or license one to do so. One must still suffer the consequences for any hurtful behavior. Moreover, the following requirements are not meant in any way to imply that you *should* necessarily like or put up with a distorted behavior that is hurtful to you. Your problem is to be aware of the price you may have to pay and to handle such behavior as wisely and harmoniously as your current Self-Esteem and Awareness permit. To do so, however, you must be aware of the *realities* involved. What is of *critical* importance in your marital relationship *is* the *realization* that your spouse could in *NO way* have done or behaved other than he or she did, or is behaving, like it or not. For your spouse CAN do ONLY what his or her prevailing Awareness caused him or her *to rather do than not do.* This realization, at a gut level, precludes resentment, ANGER, hate and bitterness, and *instead* fosters loving compassion and a heart-felt urge to "help," rather than to CONDEMN.

Furthermore, lack of these destructive emotions *enables* you to recognize and intelligently deal with the *reality* involved − in other words, to see the problem in perspective and, free of resistance and resentment, to handle it effectively as you no longer see hurtful behavior as a personal attack upon yourself. The reality IS that it isn't what happens to you, or in your life, that determines your joy or sorrow − your "feel good" or "feel bad" − *but* how you *handle it* − your attitudes and reactions, your acceptance *or RESISTANCE* of any *unwanted* reality.

1. STOP *all* value judging. Allow your partner the right and freedom of his or her own Awareness. To do so, however, you must give TOP PRIORITY for the next few weeks to achieving sound Self-Esteem. This is absolutely the most crucially important endeavor you can possibly undertake to insure a happy and fulfilling marriage relationship. For the REALITY *is:*
    (a) You cannot STOP value judging your mate until you *first* STOP VALUE JUDGING YOURSELF, and you can do this *only* to the degree that your current level of Self-Esteem permits.
    (b) You cannot make yourself "right" by making your spouse "wrong."
    (c) Your mate is *never to BLAME* regardless of his or her actions, for any fault in his or her behavior or endeavors lies not in your mate but in his or her limited or distorted Awareness.
    (d) You can allow your spouse the right and freedom of his or her Awareness only as much as you can allow *yourself* the right and freedom of *your* Awareness. And you can do this ONLY to the degree that your current *level of Self-Esteem permits.*
    (e) You can be only as kind, loving and considerate to your mate as your current degree of Self-Esteem permits.

2. Expand your Awareness of your values, NEEDS and concepts. There is a need behind EVERY voluntary action of both your own and that of your spouse. See that you discover this need and *explore* it − is it valid? Is it in alignment with Reality? What is the *source* and what are the consequences of satisfying such need? Is its fulfillment vital to your emotional well-being and/or that of your mate? Observe, question and THINK about *every* non-routine contact, condition, circumstance, situation and experience within your TOTAL environment, especially those that affect your marriage relationship. In other words, observe, question and THINK, and endeavor to understand EVERYTHING you see, think, say, do and FEEL.

3. Keep your marriage relationship in perspective. Be ever aware how much the benefits of the relationship outweigh any unwanted conditions or characteristics.

4. ACCEPT, *don't resist,* any characteristics or actions of your mate that you cannot change, even though you do not approve or like them. Be aware of the reality — your spouse has, and is entitled to, his or her own Awareness, concepts and values, however distorted you perceive them to be. The choice is yours as to how you deal with them.

5. Realize that the marriage certificate is not a "bill of sale" and that it does not convey the right to *dominate, possess* or *control.*

6. Do not find fault or condemn. COMMUNICATE — discuss any unwanted characteristic or situation openly and honestly with a clear *intent to resolve,* NOT to criticize or *accuse.*

7. Do not *demand* or *expect* anything from your mate that his or her Awareness cannot deliver.

8. Do not harbor shame, blame, guilt or remorse, regardless of the consequences of your past or current actions, and take care not to inflict blame and guilt on your mate.

9. Do not let disagreements and resentment about money or the way it is handled come between you and your spouse. Be aware that it isn't what happens, but how you handle it — your attitudes, your resistance and resentment — that causes your "feel good" or "feel bad." Recognize the realities involved and go from there.

10. Be aware of your innate authority and that you actually *are* in charge of your *own life,* and *responsible* for your own well-being — that anything worthwhile is worth working for. The choice is yours.

11. A successful marriage must be nourished and cared for. Continue to show each other the same love and consideration you did during courtship. Re-experience your thoughts, feelings, expectations and behavior that occurred during courtship and early marriage. What, exactly, has caused them to deteriorate? Were your images and expectations in alignment with Reality?

12. Certainly the basic consideration for a good marriage relationship is the "Golden Rule" — that is, treat your mate in all ways the way *you* would like to be treated. Treat each other as equals on an equal basis. Give your mate the same courtesy and freedom *you* like to be given. To do this consistently, however, you will need sound Self-Esteem.

13. Share your joys and sorrows, your work and play — your victories and defeats.

14. Do not surrender responsibility and authority for your own individual growth and well-being, *or* usurp your partner's responsibility and authority for his or her own growth and well-being.

15. Drop all masks and barriers. Be frank and open, honest and sincere with each other at all times. Do not hesitate to admit mistakes, defeats and failures. Be aware that, since you are neither your actions nor your Awareness, such mistakes cannot make you unworthy or less than, regardless of the consequences. Thus, you have nothing to hide or protect. To do this, too, you will need good Self-Esteem.

16. Be authentic — be yourself at all costs and encourage your partner to be likewise. Scrap any and ALL self-images. They restrict and interfere with your being "you."

17. Look to your own needs as well as to those of your mate. You cannot achieve sound Self-Esteem if you *feel obligated* to repress or deny your own needs.

18. Your marriage can be no better than your own sense of inner freedom and emotional well-being. The degree that you and/or your spouse lack Self-Esteem will cause emotional

turmoil and hurting.

19. Be aware of and take a genuine interest in your mate's work, hobbies and extracurricular activities.

20. Do not expect external rewards or "trade-offs" for your thoughtful and generous acts. Either the reward comes automatically in the "feel good" of the act or the particular job is better left undone.

21. Whatever you do, do not indulge in self-pity for the way you are treated by your spouse. Remember that your spouse invariably does what he or she has to do at the time and that you possess the ultimate authority and responsibility for your *own* well-being. The choice is always yours, even though you may wish to maintain the status quo rather than pay the price demanded for a desired change.

22. Do not allow marital problems to accumulate — handle them one at a time as they occur. Do not build up a head of steam that will explode at an inopportune time. Keep the "lid of the kettle cracked" so that hostility, anger and resentment can dissipate as they are generated.

23. Remember that "fair" and "unfair," "right" and "wrong" are but descriptive terms. Everyone has to do what his Awareness dictates at the time, whether you like it or not. If things become too unpleasant or intolerable, look to your partner's Awareness, not his or her actions, for a solution.

24. Do not be a "nagger" or "complainer." You cannot successfully motivate your mate through "nagging." To be constructively motivated, your mate must be made aware of the potential benefits. Actually, nagging and fault-finding motivate your mate to repudiate the "contract" rather than grow closer or nourish the relationship. Love and respect need to be nurtured, not harrassed. Thus, endeavor to resolve any resistance or resentment as it occurs, rather than resenting and complaining about it.

25. Remember that no marriage contract can be anything more than a sincere statement of intent — and is "good" only as long as an honest and caring relationship exists — as long as your needs and desires are predominantly common.

26. Do not compete with your spouse. Remember, you cannot make yourself "more than" or "less than" by your actions, no matter how superior your act or what you achieve. You can only demonstrate your current *state of Awareness*, which is no credit to you, however true to reality it may be.

27. Do not harbor resistance. If it is desirable to change something, proceed if possible to change it. If it is something beyond your power to change, accept it, knowing that situations are "what they are" and that everyone does what he has to do at the time. Consider if your mate's love or companionship is not more precious and important than the thing you resist or resent.

28. Do not harbor anger and resentment because your mate does not do what he or she "should" or "ought" to do. Your resentment stems from imposing your particular values on your mate and then resisting his or her conduct. Remember, no two people have the same Awareness and, thus, no one else in the entire world has the same system of values as you. If you think your mate is "wrong" or "unfair," in spite of being exposed to your views and values, try an alternate solution. But, do not "stew" in resentment, for your mate absolutely *has to do* what his or her current Awareness dictates, regardless of your own ideas of "right" and "wrong." Chronic anger and resentment will ruin your health and destroy your marriage.

29. A marriage requires thought and effort and a good measure of "give and take" if it is to be successful. Do not, however, deny your own needs at the expense of your Self-Esteem. There is, however, hardly anything that you cannot do for your mate, without injury to your Self-Esteem, if you will do it in the spirit of making a "gift" — an act of your own choice — instead of feeling "trapped" or forced into the action. Avoid resistance and resentment by making a "gift" of anything you might otherwise consider a duty or obligation.

30. Maintain a "clear picture" and consciousness of a happy, harmonious marriage and regularly affirm such a relationship. In any event, if your marriage is important, provide the effort and imagination required to "make it work." If it is not worth the required time and effort to nurture it, your marriage has small chance of succeeding. The choice is yours.

31. Do not use sex as a control or trading device — or merely for the quick satisfaction of a physical need. Ideally, sex is the most tender, intimate expression of your love and caring — the ultimate in togetherness. Above all, treat sex as a natural and healthy function, free of any prudery or self-consciousness.

32. Do not take your mate for granted or allow your mate to take *you* for granted. Either one is "dynamite" to a marriage.

33. Do not resist the realities of your mate's Awareness or actions. Once your emotions come into play, you are incapable of rational and effective thought or action. Do not stubbornly insist on "your rights," or on your spouse being "fair," etc., when your spouse's time, energy and/or prevailing Awareness, concepts, values, assumptions and beliefs do not permit it. The *reality* IS that you have a SELLING job to do — *not* a complaining one, for *remember,* your spouse *can* DO ONLY *what he or she would rather do than NOT do.* This is the basic Law of Human Behavior — there are NO exceptions — NONE whatever!

34. Realize that by far the greatest number of divorces and broken homes stem from an inadequate or crippling Self-Esteem. Look at its destruction all about you, and strive unceasingly to achieve and maintain *sound* Self-Esteem *if* you want to insure a rich and happy marriage.

Marriage can be a ball!

BASIC REQUIREMENTS
FOR A HAPPY AND SUCCESSFUL MARRIAGE

1. I must eliminate ALL value judging from my life. Thus,

    (1) I must STOP value judging myself on both the conscious and NON-CONSCIOUS levels.

    (2) I must STOP accepting the adverse value judgments of others.

    (3) I must PURGE my consciousness of ALL blame, shame, guilt and remorse generated by past value judgments.

2. I must perceive, accept and conform to the following five Realities:

    (1) My spouse and I are each unique and precious beings, ever doing the BEST our individual Awareness permits.

    (2) My spouse and I are each our own authority and responsible for our individual life and well-being.

    (3) My spouse and I each have the INNATE right and freedom of our own unique Awareness.

    (4) My spouse and I are both TOTALLY BLAMELESS, regardless of what either does or has done.

    (5) Should either of us commit an unwise or hurtful act, THAT one is deserving of the other's loving compassion rather than condemnation, anger, resentment, bitterness, hate or revenge.

It is clearly apparent from the foregoing Realities that there is absolutely NO *valid* justification for getting *angry, resentful* or *bitter* toward your spouse, regardless of what your spouse does or fails to do.

You, of course, do not have to *like* everything your spouse does, and you may choose NOT to put up with it if you cannot motivate your spouse to do otherwise. But, being free of mutually hurting emotions, you can deal with the particular problem objectively and effectively.

MARRIAGE ENRICHMENT AFFIRMATIONS

1. You and I are each unique and precious beings, ever doing the best our individual Awareness permits, ever growing in Awareness and love.

2. You and I are each our own authority and responsible for our individual lives and well-being.

3. You and I each have the innate right and freedom of our own unique Awareness.

4. You and I are both TOTALLY blameless, regardless of what either does or has done.

5. Should either you or I commit an unwise or hurtful act, THAT one is deserving of the other's loving compassion, rather than condemnation, anger, resentment or revenge.

6. I communicate with you openly and lovingly, for I have no self-image to PROTECT, no need for your APPROVAL, no need to CONTROL you, nothing to HIDE, nothing to PROVE, nothing to DEFEND, nothing to FEAR or RESIST, and nothing to feel GUILTY about.

7. I hold YOU blameless, for I now KNOW that you have invariably done the very best you possibly could at the time.

8. I realize we are each precious and blameless, each doing the best our prevailing Awareness permits, each growing in Awareness and love.

9. My love flows freely, for I allow you the innate right and freedom of your own unique Awareness.

10. I am thankful for your love and companionship. I accept and love you unconditionally, for I now realize that you DO HAVE the innate right and freedom of your own unique Awareness.

11. I love and cherish you because you are YOU — a unique and precious being, ever doing the best your current Awareness permits, ever growing in Awareness and love.

IT TAKES TWO TO TANGLE

Tom and Mary are continually arguing and fighting. Why? Because each does things the other thinks he or she *"should"* or *"should not"* do. What is the problem? There are two problems and two antagonists:

1. Value judging each other, and
2. Resisting each other's values and actions.

Just how *do* you get mad or angry?

1. You fail to exercise your *innate* authority to reject your mate's value judgment, and instead, resist and resent your mate for making it.
2. You feel frustrated and trapped in your mate's recrimination and blame, and endeavor to justify yourself through anger and/or retaliation.

In other words, you resist your mate's value judging or actions until you get so upset that you feel you "have really had it" and consider yourself fully justified in getting angry — and forthwith *choose* to do so, either consciously or *non-consciously*. And away you go, hammer and tongs, with no chance whatever of considering the problem calmly and objectively.

What are the realities involved in such an argument or fight?

1. It takes two to tangle — that is, *two* to fight, but
2. It takes only *one* to STOP the fight.

How? By realizing and accepting (that is, stop resisting) the reality that, whether you like it or not, your mate can do *only* what he or she *would rather do than not do* — whether it is value judging or some equally destructive action.

The basic law of human behavior, which is as exact and immutable as the law of gravity, is: *"One can do ONLY what he would rather do than not do."*

What, then, is necessary to *stop* the fight or argument? For *one* of you to acknowledge the law of human behavior and stop *resisting* the other's values and actions. Owing, however, to our identification of the individual with his actions and Awareness, we usually resist, not his actions, but the individual *himself*. This is what causes us to get so mad at the other *person* rather than at his values or actions. The message is: "You *SHOULD NOT* have *said* (or *done*) what you just did!" Therein lies the problem, for a fight always boils down to value judgments expressed in thoughts and feelings of "should," "ought" or "must."

However, if you stop resisting the other TOTALLY, the argument or fight ceases, for no one can possibly resist one who does not fight back. For example, you cannot strike the air with force, for the air does not resist your blow.

Now, stopping all value judging and resistance is *NOT* difficult *IF* you have Sound Self-Esteem and perceive and deeply understand the following *FOUR realities:*

1. One can do ONLY what his prevailing Awareness *causes him to rather do than not do*.
2. One is *neither* his actions *nor* his Awareness.
3. One can act *only* as wisely and harmoniously as his prevailing Awareness — *his current values and needs* — permits.
4. Any fault in one's behavior or endeavors lies not in the individual but in his prevailing Awareness, for which he is in *no way* to blame.

Herein lies the clue to harmonious and loving relationships, for it is clear from the foregoing Realities that ALL value judging is not only fallacious, but absolutely ridiculous!

Thus, two adults fighting is like two children playing a game in which each tries to prove the other the worse. This is truly ridiculous, for *everyone* is totally alright *exactly as they are*, for any fault or problem lies not in the individual but in his or her prevailing Awareness. One mate cannot possibly be "better" or "worse" than the other because their very existence *proves* their *innate* worth and importance. If one *does* do something the other thinks he or she "should NOT do," any problem lies in the prevailing Awareness of either one or both mates. Actually both, for as we have shown above, one cannot possibly carry on a fight *ALONE*.

Now that we see that all value judging is both invalid and foolish, how can we *STOP IT?* What is the *ONE* and *ONLY* thing you have to do to eliminate or avoid fighting with your mate? It is really very simple when you perceive and understand it. Is this not the solution? Allow each other the *right and freedom* of his or her prevailing Awareness and do *NOT RESIST* the other's values or actions. For one *HAS TO DO* whatever he or she does at the time. There are *NO* exceptions — NONE whatever! It is just as simple as taking off your coat — or *any other* voluntary act. However, owing to our faulty conditioning, it does take a certain amount of time and effort to stop value judging on both the conscious and *non-conscious* levels.

But when you can do this, you can then resolve any remaining problems free of destructive emotions and in a calm and effective manner. For, REMEMBER, you cannot possibly get angry, bitter or resentful with your spouse *IF* you acknowledge the reality that *EVERYONE* has his own unique Awareness and allow your mate the INNATE right and freedom of his or her prevailing Awareness. Again, there are *NO* exceptions — NONE whatever. But to do this you will need Sound Self-Esteem.

What is another crucially important point that is now apparent? That if you want your mate to do something, you have a job of *motivation*, NOT one of *recrimination and nagging*. Value judging and resisting actually intensify the problem, for, REMEMBER, the law is — *"One can do ONLY what he would rather DO than NOT DO."* There is absolutely NO other reason possible for doing ANYTHING!

So if you want a happy, harmonious relationship, get into alignment with reality — recognize and acknowledge this fundamental law of human behavior: "One can do ONLY what he would rather do than not do." There is NO other way to harmony and wise action, for a *law* keeps right on working whether or not you believe in and accept it. And ONLY to the degree that your Awareness IS in alignment with reality CAN you be harmonious, happy and successful in both your relationships AND throughout your life and affairs.

Now if a problem still exists, even though you have eliminated or precluded the emotional factor, there are two alternatives:

1. You can try to motivate your mate to do what you want, not through value judging and recrimination, but through open, honest communication — with a clear intent to resolve — *NOT* to prove yourself *RIGHT*.

2. Appraise your total relationship and determine whether or not the total benefits outweigh the price you must pay for them — and proceed accordingly.

BE AWARE:

1. No one is to blame, for *everyone* inevitably *HAS TO DO* what his prevailing Awareness determines he would rather do than not do. So if you want peace and harmony — if you want LOVE, in place of resentment and bitterness — you must forego all recrimination and STOP all *value judging* and *RESISTING*.

2. You *and* your mate are EACH entitled to the right and freedom of your own unique Awareness. And neither of you can avoid doing what that Awareness indicates you would rather do than not do.

3. Should you decide to separate, be aware of the TOTAL price you must pay. Ask yourself, "Just how much would my mate's behavior upset me if I did not *value judge* and *RESIST* him or her — if I allowed him or her the right and freedom of his or her Awareness?"

4. If you really want your relationship to work, AFFIRM:

OUR LOVE FLOWS FREELY BECAUSE WE ALLOW EACH OTHER THE INNATE RIGHT AND FREEDOM OF OUR OWN UNIQUE AWARENESS.

THE CHOICE IS YOURS — you can choose happiness or unhappiness. If you choose to forego value judging and resistance, then and then only, a miracle will happen — for the entire relationship changes from one of *not loving* to one of *conscious loving*. For genuine, meaningful, *demonstrable* love *IS* total, unconditional acceptance of the other — of his or her values and actions — of his or her *TOTALITY!*

DEFINITION, SIGNIFICANCE AND BENEFITS OF SOUND SELF-ESTEEM

Self-Esteem is an EMOTION. It is the degree to which you actually feel warm and loving toward YOURSELF. Thus, it follows that SOUND Self-Esteem is GENUINE LOVE OF SELF.

Lack of sound Self-Esteem is the fundamental reason one does not "FEEL GOOD" about oneself and about life in general.

Lack of Self-Esteem is the root cause of practically every personal problem that plagues one.

Lack of Self-Esteem destroys one's natural confidence and exuberance — it makes one feel inferior, inadequate, unworthy and anxious.

Lack of Self-Esteem causes depression, self-hate, resistance, resentment and bitterness.

Lack of Self-Esteem generates anxiety and fear, and denies one a sense of inner freedom, self-sufficiency and competence — of being on top of one's life and affairs!

Lack of Self-Esteem prevents exercise of one's innate authority and freedom, and causes one to hide behind protective masks and barriers.

Lack of Self-Esteem makes one feel vulnerable to the attitudes and opinions of others — desperate for their agreement and approval — a name-dropper and "people-pleaser"!

Lack of Self-Esteem causes jealousy, envy, malicious gossip, spiteful behavior and a compulsive need to be "better than."

Lack of Self-Esteem prevents close loving relationships with one's spouse, children, parents and in-laws.

Lack of Self-Esteem prevents rich, meaningful friendships.

Lack of Self-Esteem seriously handicaps one in his or her chosen occupation. It causes one to be either self-effacing and withdrawn OR compulsively aggressive and fiercely competitive.

Lack of Self-Esteem robs one of inner peace and lasting happiness.

Above all, lack of Self-Esteem denies one the love of self, of loving and being loved. As such, it fosters practically all anti-social behavior and even war itself.

Lack of Self-Esteem is self-perpetuating. Children yet unborn will suffer its torments.

With sound Self-Esteem you will not be ignored, self-conscious, timid or withdrawn. You will be free of resentment, animosity, hate and bitterness.

With sound Self-Esteem you will have no need to be fiercely competitive and aggressive in a desperate effort to prove your worth and importance — to prove yourself "better than."

With sound Self-Esteem you will allow yourself the freedom to be "less than perfect" — to goof off — free to accept mistakes, defeats and failures without being "wiped out" — without feeling unworthy or "less than."

With sound Self-Esteem you will recognize and accept your innate authority to do as you, yourself, see fit, and assume responsibility for your own life and well-being.

With sound Self-Esteem you will be able to release your full potential for creativity and happiness and to undertake any endeavor without fear of failure or defeat.

With sound Self-Esteem you will enjoy harmonious and loving relationships with your spouse, family and friends, for you will no longer be judgmental, harsh and demanding of others.

With sound Self-Esteem you will not be bored or lonesome, even when alone with yourself, for you will LIKE yourself and enjoy your own company.

With sound Self-Esteem you will no longer experience a need for the confirmation or approval of others — or a need for their attention and acceptance.

With sound Self-Esteem you will no longer have a need to impress others with your worth and importance, for you will realize that you ARE innately a unique and precious being, regardless of your achievements or lack thereof.

With sound Self-Esteem you will feel warm and loving toward yourself and warm and friendly toward all you meet — no longer hostile, suspicious, fearful or uptight.

With sound Self-Esteem you will have more true friends than you can find time for, because, being nonjudgmental, you will be both loved and loving.

With sound Self-Esteem you will enjoy a deep sense of confidence in your ability to take on anything or anybody and not worry about the outcome.

With sound Self-Esteem you will be free of self-accusation, shame, guilt and remorse. You will no longer be harsh and demanding with yourself, for you will have stopped value judging and condemning yourself.

With sound Self-Esteem you will be at ease among strangers and others regardless of their position, wealth or prestige, or lack thereof.

With sound Self-Esteem you will be happy and at peace with yourself — free of emotional turmoil and hurting, immune to the critical attitudes and adverse judgments of others — invulnerable to "put downs" and insults.

With sound Self-Esteem you will intensely enjoy the rich, meaningful "here and now" instead of existing in the barren "then and there," ever waiting for your "ship to come in" in order to be happy.

With sound Self-Esteem you will no longer be plagued with a sense of futility and frustration, for you will be organized, efficient and effective.

With sound Self-Esteem you will experience a deep sense of belonging, of harmony and oneness with your fellowmen — a tremendous zest for life, eager to get on with the exhilarating job of living, for your life will be rich and meaningful.

With sound Self-Esseem you will be respected and admired for being in active, capable charge of yourself and your affairs.

With sound Self-Esteem you will be free of fear and anxiety — of unwanted compulsive habits.

With sound Self-Esteem you will experience a tremendous overriding sense of freedom and exhilaration — a joyful eagerness to meet life on its own terms.

REALITIES OF "WILL," "FREE WILL" AND "WILL POWER"

It is apparent from the following that most of us have been burdened with false and damaging concepts of "will."

In assessing the validity of the following points, be aware that one is not his Awareness — that his Awareness is simply the CLARITY with which he perceives, understands and evaluates EVERYTHING that affects his life, and that it is the AUTOMATIC product of his heredity, total life experience AND intuitional insights.

Thus, at any given instant one's Awareness simply is what it IS. Consequently, one is rationally entitled to neither credit NOR blame for his degree of Awareness.

"FREE WILL" simply means that one is free to choose to do anything he WANTS, within his physical and inherent capabilities. What the individual wants or chooses, however, is determined by his prevailing Awareness, for no decision can be made in a vacuum — that is, without reference points or means of evaluating the pros and cons of the proposed act. Thus, despite one's "free will," he can act only as "good" or wisely as his prevailing Awareness permits.

"WILL" or an "ACT OF WILL" is simply a decision to act (that is, a free choice to act in a certain way) generated by the individual's prevailing needs or desires.

"WILL POWER" is simply the intensity of the need or desire that generated the will or decision to act in a particular way. Thus, "will power" would be more aptly termed "desire power."

"MOTIVATION" is simply one's dominant need at the time — that is, the need or desire that causes or motivates one to act in a certain way — to "rather do it than not do it." Such motivation, as well as its intensity, is determined by one's prevailing Awareness and, thus, NO ONE is entitled to EITHER credit or blame for a "strong" or "weak" will.

"SHEER WILL POWER" or "SHEER ACT OF WILL" are simply descriptive terms for one's exceptionally intense motivation or need. Thus, any "will power" or lack of "will power" lies not in the individual but in his prevailing Awareness which determines both his dominant need and its intensity.

"LAZINESS" is lack of sufficient motivation to do what you or others consider the "lazy" individual "should" or "ought" to do. It is usually a value judgment and, like all value judgments, totally invalid, for one can do only what his prevailing Awareness determines he would "RATHER DO THAN NOT DO." Contrary to general opinion, EVERYONE is MOTIVATED to do what he or she is doing or not doing at the time.

PROCRASTINATION is simply insufficient motivation to carry through with some action you or others think or feel is desirable or necessary.

"COURAGE" and "BRAVERY" are socially agreed terms to describe a certain type of motivation. Consequently, a "brave" or "courageous" individual is entitled to neither praise nor adulation, for EVERYONE literally "has to do" what his prevailing Awareness indicates is most desirable under the particular circumstances. In other words, one can do ONLY what his Awareness determines he would "rather do than not do" under the circumstances, be it "good," "bad" or indifferent.

"COWARDICE" is likewise simply a manifestation of one's Awareness and thus, a "coward" is no more entitled to censure than a "hero" is entitled to commendation and adulation.

FEAR is also a product of one's prevailing Awareness and thus, NO ONE is rationally entitled to condemnation or blame for being fearful.

WILL TRAINING: All that is necessary to "train the will" is to program yourself to be deeply aware of both the potential benefits and the total costs of the proposed action. For, regardless of any obligation or responsibility — of ALL "oughts," "shoulds" and "musts" — one can do ONLY what he would rather do than not do. There is no other reason possible for doing ANYTHING.

It is apparent from the foregoing that everyone is TOTALLY BLAMELESS — that all self-accusation, shame, blame, guilt and remorse are completely invalid — for any fault in one's motivation, behavior or endeavors lies NOT in the individual, but IN his PREVAILING AWARENESS.

BREAKTHROUGH IN AWARENESS

1. You are not your mind or body — you are that non-physical essence which animates your mind and body.

2. There is no one in the entire world one iota more or less worthy, more or less important than your own precious self.

3. You need not validate or prove yourself, for your very existence proves your innate worth and importance.

4. Your own life and well-being are your number one responsibility and you have the INNATE authority to discharge that responsibility. The better you satisfy your own needs, the more able and willing you are to serve the needs of others.

5. You actually ARE in charge of your own life and well-being, for you cannot avoid the consequences of ANYTHING you think, say, do or FEEL. You, therefore, have the authority to initiate and determine those consequences.

6. You are NOT your Awareness — you are that non-physical essence which is aware. Your Awareness is the CLARITY with which you perceive, understand and evaluate EVERYTHING that affects your life.

7. You are entitled to neither credit nor blame for your Awareness, for at any given instant it simply is what is IS — the AUTOMATIC product of your heredity, intuitional insights and total life experience.

8. You can be free and happy only to the degree that your Awareness is in alignment with reality — with what IS.

9. Your Awareness is unique, for no one else in the entire world has the same heredity, intuitional insights and total life experience as you.

10. You have the INNATE right and freedom to express your own unique Awareness, regardless of your actions or their consequences.

11. You can act only as "good" or wisely as your prevailing Awareness permits. For it is your Awareness that determines what you would rather do than not do, and this is the only reason possible for doing anything.

12. You are FREE to do anything you WANT — anything within your inherent and physical capabilities — but what you WANT is determined by your prevailing Awareness.

13. You are INESCAPABLY RESPONSIBLE for EVERYTHING you think, say, do and feel, for however limited or distorted your Awareness and regardless of what it causes you to do, or NOT do, you inevitably benefit or suffer according to the consequences.

14. You inevitably do what you HAVE to do at the time, for you can ONLY do what your prevailing Awareness determines you would rather do than NOT do.

15. You invariably do the BEST you can possibly do at the time, for you can do ONLY what your prevailing Awareness motivates you to do.

16. YOU are ALL RIGHT — *totally blameless* — *just as you ARE* — regardless of your actions, for any fault in your behavior or endeavors lies not in you, but in your *prevailing AWARENESS.*

17. Both your needs and the means you choose to satisfy them are determined by your prevailing Awareness.

18. Your fundamental need and ultimate motivation is to "feel good" mentally, physically and emotionally, or as good as the prevailing circumstances permit.

19. You can do ONLY what you most WANT to do — that is, what you *would rather do than not do*, for your basic need is to "feel good." There is no other reason possible for doing ANYTHING.

20. Your dominant need — that is, your motivation — is determined by your prevailing Awareness, for it is your Awareness that determines what you would *rather do than not do* at any given instant.

21. You CAN do ONLY what you are motivated to do — that is, what you would rather do than not do — what you THINK will make you feel BEST under the prevailing circumstances. You can do absolutely NOTHING simply because you or others think or feel you "should," "ought" or "must."

22. Your every act is an attempt to fulfill your fundamental need and basic drive — your basic drive to "feel good" mentally, physically and emotionally.

23. You are NOT your actions — you are the non-physical essence which CHOOSES and ACTS. Your actions are simply the MEANS you choose to satisfy your dominant needs. You are NOT "bad" if you ACT "bad."

24. You cannot prove your worth by your achievements, for you are NOT your actions.

25. You must pay the price determined by the total demands and unwanted consequences of your act — for EVERYTHING you do or do NOT do.

26. If you are to act wisely — that is, in alignment with reality — you must accurately weigh the potential benefits of your proposed act against the total price demanded.

27. Any mistakes, defeats or failures cannot make you unworthy or "less than," for you are NOT your actions or Awareness and can act only as wisely as your prevailing Awareness permits.

28. Despite any unacceptable, destructive or hurtful acts, YOU, yourself, *are ALL RIGHT* and deserving of compassion and love, rather than condemnation, resentment, hate or bitterness, for you have the INNATE right and freedom to act as your own unique Awareness motivates you to act.

29. There is no logical basis for pride, for you can do ONLY what your natural abilities and unique Awareness ENABLE you to do.

30. All praise and blame, all reward and punishment, are TOTALLY invalid, for you can do ONLY what your own unique Awareness motivates you to do. There are NO exceptions.

31. There are ONLY wise and unwise acts, depending on whether or not the acts are in alignment with reality. "Right" and "wrong," "moral" and "immoral," "good" and "evil," "fair" and "unfair" can be no more than descriptive terms for specific acts or behavior, for you *can do* ONLY what your own unique Awareness causes you to *rather do than not do.*

32. If you are to change your behavior, you must undergo a change in Awareness in order to change or resolve your dominant needs, OR the means you choose to satisfy them.

33. Your ONLY limitation is your LIMITED Awareness and the only cause of a deliberately hurtful or anti-social act is a DISTORTED Awareness.

34. Genuine success is "feeling good," for that and only that is fulfillment of your fundamental and ultimate need to "feel good."

35. You cannot consciously improve or expand your Awareness unless so motivated by your PREVAILING Awareness.

36. There is no valid justification whatever for self-accusation, shame, blame, guilt or remorse, for you can do ONLY what your own unique Awareness permits, and you are neither your Awareness or subject to any blame for it, however limited or distorted it may be.

37. It is not what happens in your life but your relative freedom from guilt and resistance that determines your degree of "feel good" or "feel bad."

38. There is no justification for impatience, frustration, guilt or a sense of inadequacy, for despite the intensity of your needs and desires, you can do ONLY what your time, energy and prevailing Awareness permit.

39. All personal comparisons are totally invalid as a gauge of your worth or what you "should" do or "be able to do," for no one else in the world has the same Awareness — the same needs, values, concepts, beliefs, assumptions, drives, pressures, concerns, talents and capabilities — to motivate and/or enable them to achieve or behave in a certain way.

RESISTANCE: THE ROOT OF ALL "EVIL"

The basic cause of unsatisfactory and disruptive personal relationships is that we identify each other by our actions and/or Awareness — that is, if you act "bad," you ARE "bad." We then value judge and resist the other for saying or doing something our individual Awareness does not sanction. The REALITY IS that an individual cannot possibly avoid doing what his unique Awareness determines he "would rather do than not do," regardless of what we or others think he "should" or "should not" do.

In other words, we fail to perceive or realize that the other has a different Awareness and, therefore, different concepts, values, assumptions and desires dictating everything he does. And that it is not the individual but his Awareness and actions that cause our destructive value judging and resistance, for the individual is literally forced to do what his prevailing Awareness determines he would rather do than not do.

In short, resistance arises from our limited or distorted Awareness that causes our unwillingness and, therefore, our INABILITY to allow the other the innate right and freedom of his or her unique Awareness — that is, to let it be, just as you allow the daylight and dark to be.

Following are some specific realities that illustrate the destructive consequences of resistance:

1.   The cause of practically ALL human ills is self-rejection which stems from value judging and resistance which are generated by an Awareness that is out of alignment with reality.

2.   You can accept and genuinely love yourself ONLY to the degree that you stop value judging and resisting yourself, for love IS total, unconditional acceptance. And you can stop value judging and resisting yourself and others ONLY to the degree that your Awareness (your concepts, values, needs and assumptions) are in alignment with reality.

3.   You can accept and love OTHERS only to the degree that you accept and love yourself, for you can stop value judging and resisting others ONLY to the degree that you stop value judging and resisting yourself. Value judging and resisting are diametrically opposite of loving. Since love IS total, unconditional acceptance, value judging and resistance preclude or destroy genuine love.

4.   You CANNOT POSSIBLY hurt emotionally without resisting an unwanted reality. There is just no other way to hurt emotionally.

5.   You CANNOT POSSIBLY get angry, resentful or bitter toward another without value judging that individual and then resisting him for not doing what you think or feel he "should" or "should not" have done.

6.   You CANNOT POSSIBLY avoid feeling warm and loving toward anyone you accept TOTALLY and unconditionally.

7. You can no more receive good will and cooperation from someone you are value judging than you can catch flies with vinegar. Conversely, no one can withstand your total, unconditional acceptance even though you may not like or approve of that individual's actions or behavior.

8. The only way we can claim the "feel good" which is our birthright is to stop all value judging and resisting of ourselves and to stop admitting and resisting the value judgments of others.

9. You cannot grieve for the passing of a loved one unless you are resisting the death and/or absence of the loved one. For loneliness, self-pity, anger and resentment are ALL rooted in resistance.

10. While acceptance of an unwanted reality allows that reality to change, RESISTANCE to an unwanted reality keeps one locked in and prevents one from being free.

11. It is not unwanted conditions or circumstances that make you "feel bad" but the degree to which you resist them.

12. It is not the threat to your "feel good" that makes you anxious or fearful but your resistance to that threat. If you want to free yourself of such fear or anxiety, determine what is the worst that could possibly happen to you, be willing to accept it (for if it IS going to happen, it will happen whether or not you resist it) and dismiss it from your mind.

13. Many hurtful physical tensions such as headaches and neck and shoulder aches are caused by emotional resistance. If you cannot eliminate the cause of your resistance, you CAN rid yourself of the hurting tension by agreeing to accept the unwanted situation or condition and simply let it be — just as you let the mountains and trees be.

14. The root of all emotional hurting and anti-social behavior is self-rejection and resistance to that rejected self and its actions. Self-rejection itself is caused by constant exposure to the value-judging society in which we live.

15. You are ALL RIGHT just as you ARE, for everyone is TOTALLY BLAMELESS since any fault in one's behavior or endeavors lies not in the individual but in his or her prevailing Awareness.

16. The only hope for a world without hatred, mental and physical disease, alchoholism, drug addiction, crime and WAR ITSELF is total, unconditional acceptance of one's self and others. For this IS love, and the most essential need for our emotional and physical "feel good" is to love and be loved. People who genuinely love themselves will not DELIBERATELY HURT another, let alone murder or kill each other.

SENSE AND NO SENSE

You cannot screw up your destiny — you can only postpone it.

You can't unscrew the unscrutable when you resist the rules of the game.

The only real difference between saints, sinners and wise men is the level of their Awareness.

You can't make a horse drink but you can sure get soaked trying.

Everyone has a right to hurt — to suffer the consequences of his mistakes.

Lots of money doesn't make you happy — it only makes happiness harder to come by.

Dying must be okay — everyone is doing it — some faster than others.

A hole is not always something to fill up.

If someone does not like the flowers in your garden, let him play in his own garden.

A weed is a weed is a weed — is what you think is a weed. It might make a terrific salad.

Do not knock the fly specks — they may be the seasoning.

If the water from the spring is dirty, look not to the source but to the pipe that conveys it.

A cracked pot may still hold water.

"Unfair" is the catch-all for discontent.

A man's mind is not the source but the conveyor of wisdom.

It is not the adversities of fate that cause one to suffer but how much he resists them.

It takes but little to make a man happy, but only resistance to make him unhappy.

If you want something, do not resist not having it.

If you do not like your Awareness, send in a complaint.

What a world we would have if everyone did what everyone thinks we should!

If the multitude used your path up the mountain, it would no longer be a path.

It is not the threat to your welfare that makes you unhappy, but your resistance to that threat.

If you adjust to a sick society, what have you got?

If you choose to be unhappy, it is real easy — just resist everything you don't like.

If a one-legged man is to be content, he must learn to get along with one leg.

The distorted needs of the parents are visited on their children and on their children's children, *ad infinitum.*

You can share your Awareness but you cannot force another to accept it.

If you would give your thirsting brother a drink, it is well to make sure you have water in your jug.

Resistance cannot repair a broken dish — or a broken relationship.

Fair and unfair, moral and immoral, right and wrong, good and evil can be no more than descriptive terms. It is when you load them with values that the trouble starts.

A moral admonition is one's admission of his own inability to comply.

No matter how hard and cold blows the wind, it cannot make you remove your coat.

If you would love others, first love yourself. If you would serve others' needs, first serve your own.

If you haven't a dime, do not pile the headache powder on two nickels.

If there is only happenstance and chaos here on earth, at what point does it change to the harmonious order of the heavens?

I envied the rich man until I learned the price he paid and the value he received.

No man can be a slave without his consent.

What greater blessings than freedom, love and contentment — yet they lie within everyone's grasp.

If you would achieve your objective, chart your course and do not wander — a straight line is the shortest distance between two points.

If your ball goes in the rough, that is the only place from which you can retrieve it.

Can you imagine a fish athirst in the water?

If you have a need to suffer, enjoy it.

Does not a mistake give you enough trouble without loading it with guilt?

You may belong to the "IN" group, but does it make you more secure and happy?

A bird in the hand may be worth two in the bush, but watch your hand.

Your brain can't wear out but it can atrophy.

No one will deliberately hurt another who is not himself hurting.

If you want to louse up your "feel good," always postpone the tough jobs until tomorrow.

You want freedom — what is there you can't do?

It has been said that you can no more teach what you have not learned than you can come back from where you have not been.

Value judging does not make you a judge, but it can make you un-godly miserable.

Value judging and resistance are an impassable roadblock to love and happiness.

Think not, live not.

"THE CENTRAL REALITY OF MY EXISTENCE"

I AM AS *WORTHY* AND *IMPORTANT* AS ANYONE ELSE IN THE *ENTIRE WORLD*. I AM ALL RIGHT, *TOTALLY BLAMELESS*, JUST AS I AM. I, MYSELF, CANNOT POSSIBLY *BE ANY BETTER*, FOR *ONLY* MY AWARENESS CAN BE IMPROVED.

WHY? Because

...my very existence proves my innate worth and importance.

...I am neither my actions nor my Awareness.

...I HAVE the INNATE right and freedom to MY OWN *unique* Awareness.

...I am NOT subject to blame for a limited or distorted Awareness.

...my prevailing Awareness determines my EVERY decision and action.

...I inevitably do the BEST my prevailing and ever expanding Awareness permits.

Thus, any FAULT in my BEHAVIOR or ENDEAVORS lies NOT in ME but IN my prevailing and EVER EXPANDING Awareness.

****

MASTER AFFIRMATION

(Affirmation of My Sound Self-Esteem)

I LOVE AND CHERISH MY WONDERFUL BLAMELESS SELF. I AM A UNIQUE AND PRECIOUS BEING, EVER RESPONSIBLE FOR MY OWN WELFARE, EVER DOING THE BEST MY CURRENT AWARENESS PERMITS, EVER GROWING IN AWARENESS AND LOVE — *TOTALLY FREE* OF VALUE JUDGING, SHAME, GUILT AND REMORSE.

I GOT IT!

AFFIRMATION OF MY BIRTHRIGHT

I am aware that it is my birthright to "feel good," mentally, physically and emotionally, and I claim it, gratefully and joyfully!

I accept myself totally and unconditionally as a unique and precious being, ever responsible for my own welfare, ever doing the best my prevailing Awareness permits, ever growing in Awareness and love.

1. My very existence proves my innate worth and importance. No one in the entire world is one iota more or less worthy or important than my own unique and precious self.

2. I am neither my actions nor my Awareness and inevitably do the best my prevailing Awareness permits. For it is my Awareness that determines what I would rather do than not do and there is no other reason possible for doing anything.

3. I am all right, totally blameless, just as I am. I, myself, cannot possibly be any better, for any fault in my behavior or endeavors lies not in me but in my prevailing and ever expanding Awareness, for which I am subject to neither blame nor credit. Only my Awareness can be improved.

4. Regardless of any obligations or deadlines, I can do only what my time, energy and prevailing Awareness enable me to do. Thus, I patiently do first things first, one at a time, and do not fret about what I have yet to do.

5. No self-judgments, "goofing off," mistakes, defeats or failures can possibly make me unworthy or "less than," for I am neither my actions nor my Awareness and can act only as "good" or wisely as my prevailing Awareness permits.

6. I am my own authority and experience total freedom, for even though I must pay the price exacted for my behavior, I can do anything within my inherent and physical capabilities that I, myself, see fit — anything at all.

7. I am in charge of my own life and am fully responsible for my own welfare, for I inevitably benefit or suffer according to the consequences of *everything* I think, say, do and feel.

8. I *"feel good,"* for regardless of any mistakes, defeats or failures I accept myself totally and unconditionally. I know I am a non-physical essence and that any fault in my behavior or endeavors lies NOT in me but IN my prevailing and ever expanding Awareness.

9. I have no self-image to protect, nothing to hide, nothing to prove, nothing to defend, nothing to fear, and nothing to feel guilty about, for I am ever doing the best my current Awareness permits. I have only to BE and GROW, just as a tree has only to BE and GROW.

10. I realize that I am ever doing and experiencing what is necessary for expanding my Awareness and resist nothing I cannot change.

THE KEY TO HARMONIOUS RELATIONSHIPS

The root cause of ALL human relations problems is identification of the individual with his ACTIONS and the AWARENESS which caused such actions. Recognition and ACCEPTANCE of the following realities will preclude or resolve such problems.

You cannot possibly get emotionally upset, angry, resentful or bitter towards another individual, regardless of his opinions, attitude or actions, WITHOUT value judging and RESISTING him and his AWARENESS — that is, his concepts, values, beliefs, assumptions, needs and desires, AND his actions and reactions.

If, however, you want the benefit of harmonious and effective communications and loving personal relationships, recognize and ACCEPT the fact that the prime requisite for effective communication and harmonious relationships IS SOUND Self-Esteem — AND guide yourself accordingly. For only to the degree that you have SOUND Self-Esteem can you recognize and accept your own authority and INNATE worth and importance. And only to THAT DEGREE can you communicate openly and freely — free of a compensatory need to find fault — to value judge and resist others — free of a compulsive need for confirmation and agreement — of an intense need to dominate and control — to be ALWAYS "right."

Only to the degree that you have sound Self-Esteem can you stop being harsh and demanding of yourself — and only to this degree can you stop being harsh and demanding toward another. Only then can you accept the reality of the other's Awareness and thereby allow him to be "wrong" or "less right" than yourself. In short, you can stop value judging and resisting another and his performance only to the degree that you are able to stop value judging and resisting YOURSELF and YOUR performance.

Only to the degree that you possess sound Self-Esteem can you accept and comply with the following ESSENTIAL requirements for effective communication and harmonious relationships:

1. Recognize and ACCEPT the FACT that the other is NEITHER his AWARENESS nor his ACTIONS — that he IS SEPARATE and DISTINCT from both his actions and Awareness and that he is NOT to blame for EITHER his limited and distorted Awareness OR his unwise ACTIONS, and that, therefore, he is NOT "bad" if he acts "bad."

2. Recognize and ACCEPT the REALITY of the other's unique Awareness and acknowledge his INNATE right and freedom to express that unique Awareness as that Awareness demands. For it is his PREVAILING Awareness, that he cannot possibly change at the time, that determines his EVERY decision and action.

3. Recognize and ACCEPT the FACT that the other's Awareness — his values, pressures, needs, concepts, beliefs and assumptions — IS REALITY and that he literally HAS TO DO what his prevailing Awareness indicates HE WOULD RATHER DO THAN NOT DO at the time — that he cannot POSSIBLY do OTHERWISE with his PREVAILING Awareness.

4. Recognize and ACCEPT the FACT that all value judging is totally irrational and do not VALUE JUDGE and RESIST the other for what HE THINKS, SAYS, DOES OR FEELS, for this is the REALITY of his PREVAILING Awareness and cannot possibly be changed at any given instant.

161

5.   Recognize and ACCEPT the REALITY that any fault in the other's behavior or endeavors lies NOT in HIM but IN his PREVAILING and EVER EXPANDING Awareness, and treat him accordingly.

6.   Realize that you are value judging and resisting NOT the individual, BUT his ACTIONS and the AWARENESS (for which he is in no way to blame) which CAUSED such actions. This realization takes the problem that seemed so PERSONAL and makes it IMPERSONAL. You can then deal with it calmly and intelligently, free of distorting emotions that would otherwise keep you from focusing in clearly on the problem.

This does not mean that you have to like the other's CHARACTERISTICS, or agree with his values, etc. It simply means that you accept his Awareness as the REALITY it actually IS, AND let it BE — just as you let the sun, moon and stars BE. Neither does it mean you HAVE to condone or TOLERATE the other's undesirable BEHAVIOR. Not being emotionally upset, however, enables you to deal with the individual and the problem harmoniously and effectively, for you will be free of hostility and resistance, of animosity, resentment and bitterness.

Be aware that value judging is, in effect, telling the other that he SHOULD have a DIFFERENT Awareness. This IS, of course, not only IMPOSSIBLE but RIDICULOUS, since one's Awareness is the AUTOMATIC product of his heredity, total life experience, AND intuitional insights — NONE OF WHICH he can change at the time.

Again, REMEMBER that VALUE JUDGING and RESISTING (the direct OPPOSITE of love, which IS total unconditional ACCEPTANCE) prevent open, honest COMMUNICATION, AND absolutely PREVENT or DESTROY harmonious and LOVING relationships.

It is of vital importance to your Self-Esteem and, therefore, to your emotional well-being to be EVER AWARE that you can refrain from value judging and resisting ONLY to the degree that your PREVAILING AWARENESS and SELF-ESTEEM PERMIT, AND that you ALLOW yourself the FREEDOM to value judge and resist. Otherwise, your Self-Esteem will suffer because you will value judge and resist yourself for continuing to value judge and resist others.

AFFIRMATIONS FOR A HARMONIOUS AND LOVING RELATIONSHIP

I realize that any emotional upset, any anger, resentment, hate or bitterness, stems from value judging and resisting one another, and that all value judging and resistance is caused by identifying one another with our Awareness and the actions stemming therefrom. Realizing that it is not YOU, but your AWARENESS, which upsets me makes the problem impersonal and thereby enables me to handle it intelligently and effectively, free of the destructive negative emotions stemming from value judging and resistance. I therefore affirm the following realities:

1. I realize that you, _____, are a non-physical essence, totally separate and distinct from your actions and Awareness, and that you are invariably doing the BEST your prevailing Awareness permits.

2. I refrain from value judging and resisting you, _____, for I realize that, regardless of your actions or their consequences, and even though I do not like it, you are INEVITABLY doing WHAT YOU HAVE TO DO at the time.

3. I have no need to dominate, control or resist you, _____, and I acknowledge your innate right and freedom to express your own unique Awareness as that Awareness dictates.

4. I accept and love you, _____, totally and unconditionally, as the unique and precious being you are. I realize that you are all right, totally blameless, just as you are.

I realize, however, that I can keep from value judging and resisting you ONLY to the degree that my prevailing level of Self-Esteem enables me to refrain from value judging and resisting MYSELF. And since I value a harmonious, loving relationship with you, I make every effort to achieve and maintain sound Self-Esteem.

I realize that when we refrain from value judging and resisting one another, we can resolve any conflicting needs effectively and harmoniously, free of emotional upset and with genuine love and caring for one another.

NOTE: If you do not have a Self-Esteem Index of 90 or better, we urge you to attend a Workshop for Building Sound Self-Esteem. You will be glad you did, because it will enable you to enjoy genuinely loving relationships with your mate, your children, parents, in-laws, boss, co-workers, friends and associates. For you will find that with sound Self-Esteem, success and happiness ARE INEVITABLE.

THE SUCCESS THAT REALLY COUNTS

Man's basic need is to "FEEL GOOD" mentally, physically and emotionally. Thus, no matter how much money, power and prestige he acquires, if he does NOT FEEL GOOD about himself and life in general, he has, by definition, FAILED, for he has failed to satisfy his basic need. I know, because I've been there. I was constantly hurting inside, despite my cheerful mask and international recognition as a highly successful industrialist. What good are wealth, power, prestige and fame if you are too miserable to enjoy them? I had to learn the hard way that an individual can truly enjoy the wonder and richness of life only to the degree that he feels genuinely warm and loving toward himself — when he recognizes and appreciates himself as the unique and precious being he actually is. I had to learn that it is one's birthright to "feel good" mentally, physically and emotionally, and that the prime essential for feeling good is Sound Self-Esteem. For Sound Self-Esteem is genuine love of self.

How can one learn to love himself?

When you accept yourself totally and unconditionally, despite your mistakes, defeats and failures, your real or fancied shortcomings and human frailties, you *automatically* feel warm and LOVING toward yourself. For love is total, unconditional acceptance. Thus, you can feel warm and loving toward yourself only to the degree that you are free of all self-accusation, of all shame, guilt and remorse stemming from a lifetime of faulty cultural conditioning. Only when you realize that all shame, blame, guilt and remorse are totally invalid can you accept yourself TOTALLY and UNCONDITIONALLY.

Do not confuse genuine love of self with egotism. This is actually a symptom of lack of Self-Esteem. If you totally accept and love yourself, you have no compulsive need — as egotistical persons have — for the attention and approval of others. With Sound Self-Esteem you are your own person, free to do as you see fit, regardless of the opinions and attitudes of others.

When you genuinely love yourself, you *automatically* love others and they, in turn, love you. How does this happen? When you are no longer harsh, demanding, critical and fault-finding of yourself, you stop being so with others. Others then *automatically* feel warm and loving toward YOU. This is not some moral platitude or vain hope. You do not have to work at "loving" — it just happens when you accept yourself totally and unconditionally. And does it ever feel good!

Regardless of how extensive your wealth, power and prestige, you cannot truly accept and love yourself if you feel crushed and guilt-ridden, unworthy or "less than."

Over 80 per cent of the people fired in business and industry are not terminated because of inferior intelligence or lack of ability to fulfill their assigned responsibilities. They are let go because of their inability to get along harmoniously with their supervisors, co-workers or the personnel under their supervision. With Sound Self-Esteem these individuals would not have been fired, for they would no longer have had a need to indulge in fault-finding and adverse value judgments of others. Loving themselves, they would no longer experience resentment, hate and bitterness in their personal relationships — at home AND at work.

Freedom from the emotional turmoil and hurting generated by low Self-Esteem, and its associated shame, blame, guilt and remorse, releases your tremendous inborn potential for imaginative and efficient discharge of your responsibilities. You are then able to solve any problem intelligently and creatively, rather than being bogged down in a sense of inadequacy and hopelessness.

Harmonious relationships with your spouse and children provide the needed support for you to forge ahead in your chosen career. With Sound Self-Esteem, the heartache of a broken marriage and the alienation and rebellion of your children will not occur to stifle your potential. Unhooked from your actions and the desperate compulsive need to prove your worth by your achievements, you are free to attempt the impossible without fear of defeat or failures.

Sound Self-Esteem is essential for success. When you FEEL GOOD, you succeed in all areas of your endeavors. Instead of fighting life, you go with it because you are in alignment with reality — with what IS. Thus, in place of ulcers, migraine headaches, high blood pressure and heart attacks, you enjoy buoyant health and joyful well-being.

Essential to achieving such success is the realization that you possess free will. The reality is that, within your inherent and physical capabilities, you can do anything you want and choose to do — anything at all. However, even though you can do anything you like, you are inescapably responsible for everything you think, say, do and feel, for you are inevitably subject to the consequences of everything you do or do not do.

Since your basic need and ultimate motivation is to "feel good" mentally, physically and emotionally, you invariably do what you *think* will make you feel best under the existing circumstances — that is, what *you would rather do than not do* at the time. The data your "human computer" or brain furnishes your Awareness *indicates* what you would rather do than not do. Thus, although you, yourself, make your every choice and decision, you choose ONLY what your Awareness indicates will make you feel BEST under the prevailing circumstances. If your Awareness is out of alignment with reality, both your needs and the MEANS — that is, the actions you choose to satisfy them, will be distorted, and most likely hurtful to your over-all well-being.

Now, what is the nature and source of this Awareness which indicates what you would rather do than not do? Your Awareness, as used here, is the *degree of clarity with which you perceive, analyze, evaluate and understand, both consciously and non-consciously, everything that affects your life.* It is the *automatic* product of the following three factors: your *heredity* — that is, everything you brought into the world with you; your *total life experience*, including the impact of your environment from the time of birth; and your *intuitional insights* or *"inner knowing."* This infallible inner wisdom, ever waiting on the threshold of your consciousness, can, however, come through only to the degree that you are free of inner turmoil and emotional hurting prevalent in people with low Self-Esteem.

At the instant of any decision or action your prevailing Awareness simply is what it IS — the *automatic* product of the foregoing three factors, none of which can be changed at the instant of any decision. Thus, regardless of the destructive or hurtful consequences of your acts, *you* are never entitled to blame for your decisions or actions. With your prevailing Awareness, you inevitably do *what you have to do* at any point in time. Be aware that you can do ONLY what your prevailing Awareness indicates you would rather do than NOT do. For there is no other reason possible for doing ANYTHING.

Now, there is a price exacted for EVERYTHING you do or refrain from doing. This price is determined by the total requirements of the act, such as the time, energy and/or money expended and, equally important, having to forego other desired alternatives. Another vital price factor is any unwanted consequences of the act itself.

It is this total price that tends to keep you in alignment with reality, that keeps you from engaging in hurtful and destructive behavior, providing your Awareness is not so distorted that you are out of touch with reality.

In order to feel good about yourself and others, it is essential to realize clearly and at a deep, non-conscious level of your Awareness that *no one is to blame for anything.* Or, stated another way: *You* are *all right*, totally blameless, *just as you are.* How can this be true? Because any fault in your behavior or endeavors lies *not* in *you*, but *in* your prevailing *Awareness*, for which you are never subject to blame.

Now, are you your Awareness? Definitely not. You are that which is aware. You are the non-physical essence that animates your mind and body. Your Awareness is simply an ability — you walk, you talk, you are aware. By definition *you* are not your Awareness, for you certainly are NOT the *degree of clarity* of your perception and understanding. You are never entitled to blame for your Awareness, however limited or distorted it may be, for at the instant of ANY decision, your Awareness simply is what it IS at the time — the *automatic* product of your heredity, total life experience AND your "inner knowing" — none of which can be changed *on demand.*

Please be aware, however, that even though you are NEVER entitled to blame, since you do only what your prevailing Awareness permits, you cannot possibly escape responsibility for EVERYTHING you think, say and do. For the essence of responsibility is that you are inevitably subject to the total consequences you initiate — be they "good," "bad" or indifferent.

When you internalize this fact at a deep level of your Awareness, when you stop blaming *yourself* for your mistakes, failures and defeats, you also stop blaming *others.* You then truly love both yourself AND your fellow man, for, as we have said, love IS total, unconditional acceptance. And when you stop blaming your fellow man, he *automatically* stops blaming and starts *loving* you. Can you imagine the results of such harmonious relationships with all you contact?

Here, now, is a summation of the past, present and future realities of human behavior:

PAST: You have *invariably* done exactly what you HAD TO DO at the time — what your prevailing Awareness indicated you would rather do than not do to satisfy your dominant need. You could not possibly have done OTHERWISE. So why blame yourself? Why feel "less than," unworthy, guilty or remorseful? Is it not bad enough to suffer the undesired destructive consequences of your mistakes and unwise actions without loading yourself with a destructive and totally unjustified burden of self-condemnation, shame, blame, guilt and remorse?

168

PRESENT: You are *inevitably* doing what you HAVE TO DO *NOW*, regardless of your own or others' opinions and attitudes, of conflicting needs and values, of undesired and hurtful consequences. So why not claim your BIRTH-RIGHT and experience true success — that is, "FEELING GOOD" all the time right NOW!

FUTURE: You will *inevitably* do exactly what you have to do in ALL future situations and circumstances. So why not consciously expand your Awareness by anticipating the total price of your proposed action? This will enable you to get your Awareness and actions into alignment with reality.

PAST, PRESENT and FUTURE:
NO ONE IS EVER TO BLAME FOR ANYTHING!

It is your *birthright* to *"feel good"* mentally, physically and emotionally. With Sound Self-Esteem you *automatically* feel good about yourself — about everyone and everything — on a daily basis. For you will experience the reality that it is not the unwanted conditions and circumstances in your life that cause you to "feel bad" but how much you condemn and *resist* them.

The choice is yours. If you do not feel good, look to *your Awareness and Self-Esteem* for both the cause and the remedy. For it is Sound Self-Esteem that provides the tremendous *"FEEL GOOD"* that is *the only success that really counts.* With Sound Self-Esteem, success and happiness *are inevitable!*

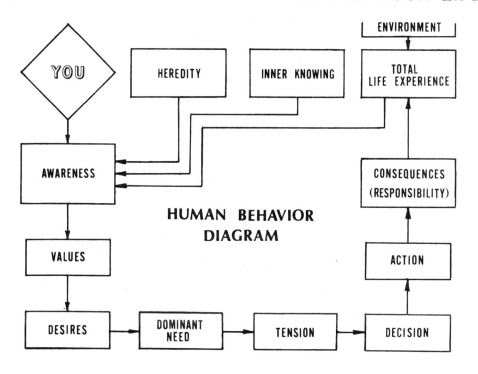

HUMAN BEHAVIOR
DIAGRAM

A thorough understanding of the role your Awareness plays in your life is essential to achieving total, unconditional acceptance of yourself as a unique and worthy individual and thus for you to reap the tremendous benefits of Sound Self-Esteem. However, in order for you to clearly understand and thereby accept the following concepts, it is essential that you maintain an OPEN MIND, one uncluttered with your present concepts, values and beliefs. It is also necessary that you do not concern yourself with any implications at this time — that you realize that the ONLY question of vital significance is: Is the particular concept true as stated? It is important that you be aware that the truth is the truth, whether or not you understand and accept it as such.

It is essential to first determine WHO "YOU" ARE, if you are to fully understand the nature and significance of your Awareness. Now just WHO ARE "YOU"?

Are "you" your mind? No, your mind is but the activity of your brain and associated nervous system. "You" are that which UTILIZES your mind — that which thinks and makes decisions. If you WERE your thoughts and decisions, you would cease TO BE any time you fell into a coma or dreamless sleep.

Are "you" your body? No, "you" are that which ANIMATES your body. You are not your body, for you can lose both arms and legs, as well as many other parts of your body without being diminished as an individual. Your body, although of vital importance to your functioning and over-all well-being and "feel good," is simply the VEHICLE or instrument *through which you function* in this material phase of your existence.

171

If "you" are neither your mind nor body, what then are "you"? Let's check. Suppose the doctor has pronounced you dead. Your body is still around, on the bed, in the coffin, or wherever. However, something has changed, for your body is now cold and rigid. Obviously, something has left, for your body can no longer move or speak. Nothing, however, has been seen to leave. What then has left? Must it not be the NON-PHYSICAL ESSENCE that INHABITED and ANIMATED your mind and body — that was aware, that made decisions and acted? Is it not this non-physical essence that left the real "YOU"?

"You," then, are that non-physical essence which *utilizes* your mind and *functions through* your body — that which is AWARE and ACTS.

Now, what do we mean by your "Awareness"?

Your Awareness, as we use the term, is the DEGREE OF CLARITY with which you PERCEIVE, ANALYZE, EVALUATE and UNDERSTAND, both consciously and *non-consciously*, EVERYTHING that AFFECTS YOUR LIFE. In short, your Awareness is simply the FUNCTIONING of your senses, of your human computer or brain and its associated nervous system.

Now what determines your Awareness? There are three factors: one, your HEREDITY — everything you brought into the world with you; two, your TOTAL LIFE EXPERIENCE from the instant of your birth, including the full impact of your lifelong ENVIRONMENT; and three, your INNER KNOWING — information which you receive intuitively. INNER KNOWING is something you KNOW you KNOW, because of an INTUITIVE FEELING that it is true, regardless of how many may tell you that you are "wrong" — something that you KNOW without the process of logical analysis and evaluation. Thus, at any given time your existing Awareness is the AUTOMATIC product of your HEREDITY, TOTAL LIFE EXPERIENCE and INNER KNOWING. Your Awareness is, therefore, UNIQUE, for NO ONE can possibly have the same heredity, total life experience or intuitional insights as you.

Now are "you" your Awareness? Definitely not.

Why? Because "you" are that non-physical essence which is AWARE, which observes, thinks and understands. You cannot be both your thoughts and the one who thinks. Your Awareness is, simply one of your abilities, like being able to walk or talk. You are certainly NOT one of your abilities or functions — you are definitely NOT how clearly you perceive, think and understand.

Are "you" your actions? No, certainly NOT.

Why? Because "you" are a non-physical essence. "You" are that which ACTS. Your actions are simply the MEANS you choose and, therefore, the ATTEMPTS you make to fulfill your dominant needs. You are NOT your actions, for you can no more be both the ACTOR and the ACT than the subject of a sentence can be both the noun and the verb of the sentence. If you were your voluntary actions, "you" would cease TO BE any time you were not engaged in some endeavor. Most of us, however, have been conditioned to identify with our actions, behavior and achievements. For example, we have been conditioned to believe that we must prove our worth through our accomplishments — and that if we act "bad," we ARE "bad."

There is, however, no evidence to support the concept that one IS his actions. Thus, since you are NOT YOUR ACTIONS, and although you cannot avoid their consequences, "you" are NOT "bad" if you act "bad."

Now are you ever entitled to praise or blame for your Awareness — for the clarity of your perception and understanding? Definitely not.

Why? Because at any point in time your Awareness simply is what it IS — the AUTO-MATIC product of your HEREDITY, TOTAL LIFE EXPERIENCE and INNER KNOWING — not one of which you can possibly change at the instant of any decision or action.

Now let us refer to the Diagram of Human Behavior to better understand the crucial role your Awareness plays in your life.

What IS so crucial about the role your Awareness plays? That it IS your Awareness that determines your every decision and action. And since your psychological and/or physical actions determine your feelings, it is your Awareness that determines whether you "feel good" or "feed bad." The fact is that you CAN "feel good" ONLY to the degree that your Awareness — your perception and understanding — IS IN ALIGNMENT WITH REAL-ITY, with what ACTUALLY IS.

Let's see how it works.

Now since your Awareness determines how you perceive, analyze, evaluate and under-stand everything that affects your life, it is your Awareness that establishes your concepts, beliefs, assumptions, aspirations, personal VALUES and NEEDS.

What do we mean by personal values? A personal value is something of SIGNIFICANT IMPORTANCE to an individual. It may be a PERSON, PLACE, THING, ACTIVITY, CON-CEPT, BELIEF, BEHAVIOR or whatever. Personal values generate desires, which in turn create needs.

What do we mean by needs? A need is an unsatisfied DESIRE intense enough to gen-erate TENSION. Such tension persists until the particular need is either fulfilled or resolved.

Now what is a DOMINANT need? Your dominant need is the need on which you act. Why? Because it is more intense than any competing needs you have at the time.

Now what is the function of this tension you experience? It is simply your SIGNAL TO ACT — your signal to satisfy the dominant need which generated it. Such tension may be physical, mental or emotional, or all three.

Why is tension a signal to act? Because man's inborn basic need is to "FEEL GOOD" mentally, physically and emotionally. Thus, if you are to satisfy this basic need, you must make a decision to act in such a way as to eliminate this uncomfortable and disturbing tension.

Now it is your Awareness — how clearly you perceive, analyze, evaluate and under-stand everything that affects your life — that advises you what to do to eliminate this unwanted tension. Thus, it is your Awareness that determines your every decision. And, as a result of such decision, you "feel good" or "feel bad" depending on the specific action your Awareness indicated would relieve this tension.

So you have made a decision and acted accordingly — that is, you have done the best your prevailing Awareness permitted to fulfill your dominant need and thereby relieve your tension. But you are not yet through with your "need cycle" — there are still the CONSE-QUENCES of your action. You are inevitably responsible for EVERYTHING you think, say, do and feel, for you cannot possibly avoid the consequences of anything you do or refrain from doing. This is the ESSENCE of RESPONSIBILITY.

These consequences become a part of your total life experience and change your existing Awareness accordingly. Thus, you benefit from such consequences in making future decisions.

Since you can dispose of only one dominant need at a time, you can now deal with your next dominant need. Thus, your need cycle starts all over again.

If your Awareness is distorted, both your needs and the means you choose to fulfill them will be distorted. Thus, it is apparent from the foregoing that you can "feel good" only to the degree that your Awareness is in alignment with reality. If, therefore, you are to "feel good" on a day-to-day basis, it is ESSENTIAL that you DO get your Awareness into alignment with reality. This, then, is your number one responsibility. For the better you fulfill this responsibility, the better you will feel toward yourself and hence the more kind and loving you will be to both *yourself* and *others* — AND *they* to *you.*

Note: You can check your understanding of the role your Awareness plays by filling in the spaces below from memory.

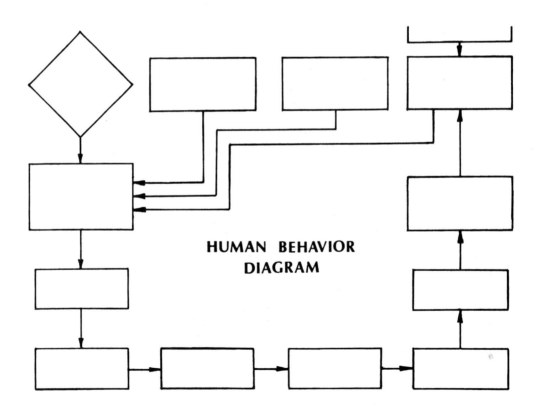

HUMAN BEHAVIOR DIAGRAM

174

NOTES

NO ONE IS TO BLAME

1. My Awareness is the degree of clarity with which I perceive, analyze, evaluate and understand, both consciously and non-consciously, *everything* that affects my life.

2. I am neither my Awareness nor am I entitled to either *credit* or *blame* for its clarity. My Awareness is but a *function* — the *degree of clarity* with which I *perceive* and *understand*. It is the AUTOMATIC product of my heredity, total life experience and inner knowing or intuitional insights — none of which factors are under my control at any given time.

3. My inborn need is to "feel good" mentally, physically and emotionally. Thus, in order to "feel good" I inevitably do what I most want to do — that is, *what I would rather do than not do* at the time. This is the only reason possible for doing ANYTHING.

4. It is my prevailing Awareness — that is, how clearly I perceive, analyze, evaluate and understand my total life experience and intuitional insights — that informs me *what I would rather do than not do*.

5. Thus, it is my *Awareness* that determines my *every decision and action.* Consequently, any fault in my behavior or endeavors lies NOT in *me*, but IN *my prevailing Awareness.*

6. Although *never to BLAME* for any faults in my behavior or endeavors, I am *inescapably responsible* for EVERYTHING I *think, say, do* and *feel*, for I cannot possibly avoid the CONSEQUENCES. This is the *essence of RESPONSIBILITY.*

LOVE AND LOVING

Love is a NATURAL state of being. The following statement is not theory; it is a demonstrable fact. LOVE IS, in effect, TOTAL, UNCONDITIONAL ACCEPTANCE, for you automatically *experience* LOVE when you accept yourself and others totally and unconditionally. For years I felt guilty when the minister solemnly entoned, "We must now all go out and love our fellowmen." Never having experienced love, I did not know what real love was. I said I loved my wife and family, and I thought I did. I now realize what I thought was love was not love at all, for it was CONDITIONAL: I love you because you are pretty, because you are generous and attentive, but mainly because you take care of my needs. Because... because...because.

What does total, unconditional acceptance mean? Total means ALL -- I accept you fully and completely; I accept you just the way you ARE, with your scars, birthmarks, faults, hangups, screwed up values, your sweetness, your sourness, EVERYTHING. In short, I accept you as freely and totally as I accept breathing in and out -- as totally as I accept the fact that I must breathe to live, as completely as I accept the sun, moon and stars.

Unconditional acceptance means just that -- acceptance free of any and all conditions, of all "becauses," "buts," "ifs" and "shoulds" -- of all demands and expectations. It means I accept you NOW, totally and unconditionally, just as you are, with no doubts or misgivings -- with no mental reservations, with no secret need to straighten you out. In my eyes you may have undesirable characteristics or shortcomings, but I accept those, too, for I accept the totality that is YOU.

Total, unconditional acceptance, however, does not mean you must like or accept another's hurtful actions or behavior. You accept the person and deal with his behavior as your prevailing Awareness indicates.

And in this total, unconditional acceptance I allow you total freedom to be you, for I have no conditions you must fulfill in order to gain my approval and acceptance. This is love -- richly meaningful, joyful love -- love with a handle. A handle anyone can take hold of to EXPERIENCE this love, right here and now, providing they have sufficient understanding and Self-Esteem to no longer have a need to value judge, to criticize and find fault. Providing they no longer need to belittle and put others down in a vain and futile effort to make themselves "right" by making others "wrong."

The only catch, however, is that in order to love and be loved by others, we must first love ourselves. We must first accept ourselves totally and unconditionally. We must first stop accusing and condemning ourselves if we are to eliminate the compulsive, compensating need to make others "wrong."

The reason we do NOT accept and love ourselves unconditionally is that we identify ourselves with our Awareness and the actions stemming from that Awareness. We, therefore, adversely value judge ourselves because of our mistakes, defeats and failures -- because of our unwise and hurtful behavior, or behavior we and/or society CONSIDER "bad," "wrong" or "immoral." We then feel "less than," unworthy and guilty. We cannot accept ourselves totally and unconditionally when we do not feel good about ourselves.

The problem is that our Awareness -- the CLARITY with which we perceive, analyze, evaluate and understand the various factors in our lives -- has been thrown out of alignment with REALITY -- with what actually IS -- by a lifetime of FAULTY CULTURAL CONDITIONING. Thus, if we are to love ourselves and others, we must get our Awareness back into alignment by eliminating the false and destructive concepts of human existence and behavior that cause us to adversely judge and resist ourselves. This re-conditioning process must start with the realization that we are neither our actions nor Awareness, and that we can act only as wisely as our prevailing Awareness permits. This is the beginning of acceptance.

Once we stop adversely value judging and resisting ourselves, we start loving ourselves. Since loving is a natural state of being, we need make no effort -- we need not even TRY to love. It JUST HAPPENS -- AUTOMATICALLY. For once we eliminate the road-blocks, the value judgments and resistance, we automatically revert to our natural state of loving. It is just that simple. All we have to do is to get rid of the false and destructive concepts that prevent total, unconditional acceptance, and LOVE becomes a living experience.

Furthermore, once we stop value judging and resisting ourselves, we eliminate our compensating need to value judge and resist OTHERS. We then revert to our natural state and begin loving others. For we then automatically accept THEM totally and unconditionally, thereby removing the roadblock to our loving them as we love ourselves.

Conversely, any time we start value judging and resisting someone we have been loving, we automatically STOP loving them to the degree that we value judge and resist them. In fact, this is what happens when "the honeymoon is over" and the young lovers become aware of the "faults" in their partners. Only as they are able to accept each other totally and unconditionally can they regain their original state of loving. If, during the rapture and ecstacy of first love, they were aware of each other's "faults" and shortcomings, they would probably never have gotten married in the first place. This is, no doubt, why "first love" is "BLIND." As a matter of fact, it is adverse value judging and resistance that causes ALL personal relationship problems -- all anger, resentment, hate and bitterness, as well as parent-child alienation and broken homes.

On the other hand, when we accept others totally and unconditionally, they cannot ignore this loving acceptance and they start loving us in return. Again, it just HAPPENS -- no one has to "go and do it."

Now one's level of Self-Esteem is the DEGREE that he accepts himself, based primarily on his sense of personal worth and importance in the scheme of things. Thus, Sound Self-Esteem is total, unconditional acceptance of himself as the unique and precious being he actually is.

We CAN, however, accept and love ourselves only to the degree that we achieve the following realizations:

1. NO ONE is MORE WORTHY OR IMPORTANT than your own unique and precious self.

2. You are inescapably responsible for EVERYTHING you do and in charge of your own life.

3. You have the AUTHORITY and total FREEDOM to express and act as you, yourself, see fit.

4. Regardless of any hurtful behavior, mistakes, defeats or failures, you are all right, totally blameless, JUST AS YOU ARE. Any fault lies not in YOU but in your prevailing Awareness.

5. You are a non-physical essence – a PRECIOUS, UNIQUE and MEANINGFUL part of a beneficent universe – ever growing in Awareness and Love.

We can achieve these realizations ONLY to the extent that we get our Awareness back into alignment with reality. This we can do by investigating our faulty concepts of human existence and behavior and replacing them with PROVEN REALITIES. Only then can we genuinely love ourselves and others, and only then can others love us. It all happens AUTOMATICALLY once we accept OURSELVES totally and unconditionally. This is where it all starts. Learning to remove the roadblocks to loving ourselves and others is the only REALISTIC hope for a better world -- a world free of hostility, hate, bitterness, greed and aggression -- of even war itself.

180

BASIC REALITIES OF BEING AND DOING

I DESERVE to "feel good," for it is my BIRTHRIGHT to "feel good" mentally, physically and emotionally. The more I get my Awareness into alignment with reality, the more I EXPERIENCE this "FEEL GOOD."

I AM the NON-PHYSICAL ESSENCE which INHABITS and ANIMATES my mind and body — which is AWARE and ACTS.

I am neither my AWARENESS nor my ACTIONS, which stem from that Awareness. Thus, I cannot PROVE, DISPROVE or IMPROVE my worth and importance by my BEHAVIOR OR ACCOMPLISHMENTS.

My very EXISTENCE proves my innate WORTH and SIGNIFICANCE. Thus, no one in the entire world IS more or less WORTHY, more or less SIGNIFICANT than my own UNIQUE and PRECIOUS self.

I AM a PRECIOUS, UNIQUE and MEANINGFUL part of Life. The world would not be the same without ME.

My every action is but the MEANS I choose to FULFILL my DOMINANT NEED.

My inborn BASIC NEED is to "FEEL GOOD" mentally, physically and emotionally.

I CAN do ONLY what I MOST WANT to do — that is, what I WOULD RATHER DO THAN NOT DO to satisfy my basic need to "feel good."

My AWARENESS determines my every DECISION and ACTION, for it is my Awareness that INFORMS me WHAT I WOULD RATHER DO THAN NOT DO.

Since my Awareness determines my every decision and action, ANY FAULT IN MY BEHAVIOR OR ENDEAVORS lies NOT in ME, but IN my prevailing Awareness, which is in NO WAY me.

There is NEVER any RATIONAL JUSTIFICATION for SHAME, BLAME, GUILT or REMORSE, for "I" am NEVER TO BLAME for any distorted or hurtful actions, for any mistakes, defeats or failures.

I am NOT "bad" if I ACT "BAD," for I am neither my actions nor my Awareness and can act ONLY as "good" or wisely as my prevailing Awareness permits.

Although totally FREE of BLAME for any faulty behavior, I am INESCAPABLY RESPONSIBLE for my physical and emotional WELL-BEING, for I BENEFIT or suffer according to the CONSEQUENCES of EVERYTHING I THINK, SAY, DO and FEEL.

I am my own AUTHORITY and IN CHARGE of my own Life and WELL-BEING, for I AM INESCAPABLY RESPONSIBLE for EVERYTHING I do or do not do.

I function in TOTAL FREEDOM, for although I MUST PAY A PRICE FOR EVERYTHING I DO, within my capabilities I CAN DO ANYTHING I, myself, see fit — anything my Awareness indicates I WOULD RATHER DO THAN NOT DO.

I cannot CHANGE my BEHAVIOR without a change in my DOMINANT NEED. This cannot be done without a change in my EXISTING Awareness.

I am inherently SELFISH, for my BASIC NEED is to "FEEL GOOD." Thus, I can DO ONLY what I think will make me "feel good," or "better" than I would otherwise feel.

My NUMBER ONE responsibility is my own LIFE and WELL-BEING. The better I love myself and take care of my own needs, the more WILLING and ABLE I am to help others.

appendix

ADDITIONAL PUBLICATIONS ON SELF-ESTEEM

BY L.S. BARKSDALE

Published by the The Barksdale Foundation
For Furtherance of Human Understanding

BUILDING SELF-ESTEEM, 1972, 42 pages (100,000 copies in print)

STUDY GUIDE FOR BUILDING SELF-ESTEEM, 1972, 45 pages

FOLLOW-UP WORKBOOK FOR BUILDING SELF-ESTEEM, 1973, 42 pages (Out-of-print)

DAILY PROGRAM FOR BUILDING SELF-ESTEEM, 1974, 24 pages (Out-of-print)

SELF-ESTEEM WORKSHOP SUPPLEMENT, 1975, 42 pages (Out-of-print)

BUILDING SOUND SELF-ESTEEM INSTRUCTOR'S GUIDE, 1978, 174 pages (Available only to Workshop Leaders)

MANUAL FOR BUILDING SOUND SELF-ESTEEM, 1978, 86 pages (Available only in Workshops)

SELF-ESTEEM WORKSHOPS

We urge you to participate in one of our Self-Esteem Workshops to further implement and internalize the concepts in this book. During the Workshop, participants are guided through a pleasant learning experience which includes thought-provoking lectures, non-threatening exercises, stimulating group discussions and contemplative moments – all designed to build and achieve Sound Self-Esteem.

These Workshops are held periodically throughout the United States, in Canada and Australia and can be arranged in your area by special request. For information on Workshops and a price list of our publications, please write:

THE BARKSDALE FOUNDATION
P.O. Box 187
Idyllwild, California 92349

ENDORSEMENTS*

(From individuals participating in Self-Esteem Workshops
and using Barksdale Foundation Self-Esteem materials)

"Thanks to your materials, the focus of my life has shifted from proving myself to enjoying myself, and I am grateful that you have been able to provide me with that help."

"This workshop was a warm and enlightening experience. The program has given me new hope for happiness. It's given me the desire to pursue and study all the information and insights the Foundation has to offer."

"Your materials, including the workshop, have been an enriching experience for me. The discovery of such simple tools for a less hurting philosophy of living is terrific. To know that my new self-love will bounce off so many people and, hopefully, entice them to taste life as I now am, is a shivering feeling. Thanks, Barks, for giving me a new look on living."

"The earth-shaking, incredibly all-encompassing basic concepts of Sound Self-Esteem boggle my mind! When applied completely and specifically to areas such as education, health care, penal codes, child rearing -- virtually every aspect of life -- the possibilities are fantastic."

"I have a feeling of 'this is too good to be true.' These materials give me much hope for a better future -- uncomplicated, easy to grasp, makes good sense. I have a feeling of 'I've finally found the TRUTH'!"

"To learn that loving myself is the key to establishing sound self-esteem, and to be given the tools to continually affirm that fact is terrific."

"Mr. Barksdale has effectively developed a program that can be applied on a large scale to laymen and professionals alike. It effectively teaches people how to raise their self-esteem base regardless of where it may be initially."

"Your Self-Esteem Workshop gave me invaluable tools that will be with me the rest of my life. I am excited about myself, who I am and what I'll become -- all because of a 'breakthrough in awareness'."

"These concepts are very positive and powerful. The step-by-step repetition of the principles and laws of reality and self-esteem leave no room for anything but a greater personal self-awareness."

"The Self-Esteem Workshop was a beautiful event of great significance to my life. I am greatly unburdened from a good part of a heavy load of negative programming that I have been carrying all my life. I am tickled that I have found a path that will continually increase my capacity for enjoyment."

"All my life I've been looking for something that made rational sense and order. This is it!"

*On file at Foundation Headquarters, Idyllwild, California

The Barksdale Foundation *For Furtherance of Human Understanding*, an independent, self-funding, non-profit institution, is the pioneer in developing effective methods and tools for building sound Self-Esteem. Its unique, educational program is currently being used successfully by thousands of individuals, by schools, colleges and universities, by hospitals, mental health institutions, private therapists, industry and religious groups throughout every state in the Union and in many foreign countries. It is also used by county, state and federal organizations and is incorporated in government-funded projects.

The study and research of the Barksdale Foundation confirms that low Self-Esteem is the major cause of practically all emotional hurting and unhappiness. The Foundation's basic endeavor is to provide individuals with the necessary information and tools to enable them to build sound Self-Esteem and thereby live happier and more constructive lives. This is accomplished in Self-Esteem Workshops, in seminars, lectures and self-led study groups, and through circulation of its booklets and tapes. Foundation Headquarters: 53625 Double View Drive, P.O. Box 187, Idyllwild, California 92349; telephone: 714/659-3858.